The Joy of Retiring

*

555 Ways
To Get a Kick
Out of Retirement

Book design by Creative Culture
Edited by Away With Words

Library and Archives Canada Cataloguing in Publication

Delorie, Oliver Luke, 1975-, author
    The joy of retiring : 555 ways to get a kick out of retirement / Oliver Luke Delorie.

ISBN: 978-0-9948468-4-6 (paperback)

    1. Retirement. 2. Retirees--Life skills guides. I. Title.

HQ1062.D456 2017   646.7'9
C2016-906185-X

For bulk orders or other enquiries please email the publisher at: SnowbirdBooks@gmail.com

Foreword

Everyone should have a list of things to do in retirement, and a good place to start is by reading this book.

Assembling your own catalog of activities will give you a profound sense of accomplishment; perhaps much more than you enjoyed at work.

So ditch the proverbial retirement 'bucket list' and create your own, using the myriad of ideas in this book as your guide.

In short, the people who enthusiastically fill up their calendars with a variety of activities wind up living life to the fullest.

This is your one-way ticket to fun.

~ Ernie J. Zelinski
Author of *How to Retire Happy, Wild and Free* (over 325,000 copies sold in 9 languages) and *The Joy of Not Working* (over 300,000 copies sold in 17 languages).

Disclaimer

This book is sold with the understanding that neither the author nor the publisher are engaged in rendering legal, psychological, medical, or any other professional advice. If such advice or other assistance is required, the services of competent professionals should be sought. Any decisions made by the reader as a result of reading this book are made at the sole responsibility of the reader, and thus the author and publisher assume no liability for any such decisions. Please enjoy responsibly.

Introduction

NOW is the time to courageously chase your dreams, face your fears, and live the life you have always imagined.

If true wealth is free time, you are a billionaire! You are free to explore and experiment and indulge in whatever activity tickles your fancy.

- What is on your bucket list?
- What did you love as a child?
- What will you regret NOT doing?

My goal is to rekindle your excitement for retirement in such a playful way that you may truly experience *The Joy of Retiring*.

Although this book (like all others) is only a map, I trust it has within it seeds that once watered will blossom into bliss.

I believe that if you speak from (and follow) your heart, you will always get where you want to go. May you find your joy in retirement.

1. Smash a Piñata

Where do you get a piñata at 2am when you don't live in Mexico? Go down to your local dollar store and buy a bag of flour, some of balloons, a ream of colorful tissue paper, and a cheap bag of assorted candy. On your way home, grab a newspaper out of your neighbor's recycling bin and the *Louisville Slugger* from the storage shed. Get the grandkids involved and you're in business.

2. Experience Zero Gravity

Ever dream of going into space? Wake up! For the price of a few mortgage payments, you can finally fly like *Superman*. And to hell with seasickness; this once-in-a-lifetime opportunity is well-worth the resulting homelessness until you get back on your feet. Though in the meantime, why not have some fun? Just imagine the possibilities.

3. Write a Novel

Everyone wants to write a book, but only 1 out of 100 do anything about it. Why? Because they are either too lazy, or don't believe they can write. If you are determined to write and publish a book, start writing. You can always spend the next 20 years rewriting it over and over again until it makes sense (if ever). Or you could just get it over with and do what 50% of authors do: hire a ghostwriter.

4. Get a PhD

Do you prefer the DR prefix before your name, or the MD suffix after it? No matter; your acronym might be mistaken for the following: *Personality Highly Deformed; Pacemaker Has Damage; Possibly Half-Dead; Person Harbors Delusions; Probably Hardened Defeatist; Post-Honorary Depression; Position Hardly Deserved.* You can thank the contributor of this book's foreword (if you must) for these light-hearted alternatives to such noble credentials.

5. Tattoo Someone's Name on Your Chest

Imagine the look on your spouse's face when they see their favorite word emblazoned on your chest in über-permanent ink. If you went down to the tattoo parlor together, neither of you likely regret your decision. But just don't go branding yourself with your online date's username until you meet them, okay?

6. Grow Your Own ... Vegetables

By hook or by crook, eek out a garden plot and ask your neighbor with the Fall Fair-winning acorn squash how to go about growing your own veggies. This green thumb will love the attention and feel like an expert when you pepper them with questions about organic vs. non-organic, planting by the moon, and saving seeds. Come harvest time, you may just find yourself in ecstasy (the legal kind).

7. Tell a Stranger You Find Them Attractive

This is both easier and harder than it sounds (all you have to do is open your mouth and not say something stupid). But opening your mouth and having something intelligent come out to an attractive stranger is likely not something that happens too often. But what have you got to lose? Nothing you can't get back. Give it a try (it just might work).

8. Hypnotize a Chicken

You can put your own (or someone else's) chicken into a trance without the use of drugs and/or dance music. For a quick 30 second fix, simply tuck the chicken's head under its wing, rock it back and forth, and put him/her on the ground. Harmless farm fun that won't get you in trouble with PETA (in case you were worried they had their eyes on you).

9. Eat Vanilla Pudding From a Mayonnaise Jar

Homemade pudding tastes better, but it's more work, so grab a spoon and go find a crowded place where you will get the most attention. Make eye contact, and keep a straight face if you can. Of course, this only works if you have a sense of humor (but maybe you need one). This will work.

10. Inhale Helium and Talk Funny

You know what happens when your brain is denied the essence of life, right? In case you missed that day of science class, helium is not oxygen. Want proof? Just ask Huey, Dewey and Louie. They'd tell you Uncle Donald was a few sandwiches short of a picnic, so don't overdo it. But temporary cartoon insanity aside, getting the giggles high on helium is a gas!

11. Take a Polygraph Test and Pass It

Most professionals agree that lie detectors can't tell the truth, so your secrets are safe for now. Still, aren't you interested to know if your closeted skeletons would make you sweat when you have everything riding on one spin of the roulette table? If not, how about vetting the questions beforehand, like the celebrity's assistants do before interviews.

12. Get Arrested for a Good Cause

What injustices boil your blood? Or to be more precise, what injustice boils your blood the most? Rest assured (like you will in prison) there are legions of eco-warriors and bra / flag / effigy-burning radicals out there waiting for you to sign a petition and stand up for what you believe in. Ever heard of *The Raging Grannies*?

13. Sponsor a Child

You've seen them on TV. And maybe you have visited a war-torn or famine-ravaged country and witnessed the immediate and desperate need with your own eyes. For less than the cost of a cup of coffee a day, you can help a child get the medicine, food and education they need to reach that stage of life known as adulthood.

14. Stay in Bed All Day on Purpose

Brush your teeth, go to the loo and grab a bowl of cereal. Now get back into bed. Yes, you will feel guilty (it's difficult to reprogram yourself) so pick a distraction (anything but TV). Now take it to the next level and turn off your phone. If you can make it past noon, you are in the clear and can start drinking stigma-free.

15. Start a Blog

There are billions of ways to do everything, so why not join the countless bloggers online and light up the information highway with words, images and sounds? Believe it or not, you can still stake your claim in cyberspace. And thanks to countless resources (online and off) you can be ranting about politics or exploiting Fluffy (for free) in less than 5 minutes.

16. Go Bowling

Could you get used to being called The King of The Lanes? Like most things in life worth the win, all it takes to become known as (at least) The Prince of Pins is a little practice. 5- or 10-pin, 'black light' bowling is where it's at. Don your best lounge lizard velour leisure suit and get cozy with every foot in your town, because those shoes have seen some action.

17. Tee Time

Where else can you start the day drinking screwdrivers with your friends; meander your way through some of the most meticulously-manicured meadows on the planet on a zippy, battery-powered, canopied go-kart; take your frustrations out on a little ball; and top it all off guffawing over barbecued steaks while neither spouse nor children are anywhere to be found? Oh yeah, and where the sun is also slowly setting in the background.

18. Go Diving

Do you hear the theme to *Jaws* whenever you put your head underwater (even in a swimming pool)? Face your fears with a snorkel, mask and flippers and lazily float the day away in a sheltered lagoon in some tropical paradise. What, too easy? You dream of staring down death-by-wild-beast in the face? At least opt for a shark-proof cage.

19. Leave a Ransom Note

What favorite possession could you safely kidnap and leave a playful ransom note for? Who would enjoy such mischief? If you don't have anyone to goof around with, go out and find someone (if only so you can take their favorite toy hostage and demand they give in to your unreasonable demands). Note: playful power struggles demand a sense of humor.

20. Crash a Party

The next time you are all dressed up with nowhere to go and just happen to be cruising (read: loitering) around your RV park or the swanky gated neighborhood next door with the best 6-pack you can afford under your arm, all is not lost. There is a party in full swing somewhere, so step out of your comfort zone and join in the fun. What if you had fun / made some friends / got turfed / arrested / laid / married? Hopefully not all in the same night, of course (unless that's how you roll).

21. Play Badminton

Ever wonder why the shuttle cocks are called birdies? It's because the real ones are made with bird's feathers (not dead birdies). If you are lucky to have a backyard, string up a net, and scrounge some rackets from a garage sale or dollar store. As long as you remember: *a bird in the hand is worth two in the bush,* you will always have ammunition to swat at your opponent.

22. Study Martial Arts

Lesson 1: Hi-Ya! Spin! Kick! Punch! Duck! Lesson 2: Breathe in as you lift your arms. Breathe out as you bend your waist. Up. Breathe. Down. Breathe. Repeat. Now, do you want to pounce on your prey like a tiger; slither up silently like a cobra coming in the for the kill; or calm your inner demons with kindness and compassion, Buddhist-style? How you attack (or defend yourself) is up to you.

23. Hang Your Own Art on The Wall

If you are you proud of your work, show it off (even if you live alone and never invite people over). Surround yourself with it. Create a cocoon of beauty and magic and proportion (or lack thereof). Let your inner world splash out into your life to inform you and guide you and delight you. If you love this idea (and you haven't already accepted the fact you are a narcissistic creative genius) you don't need further encouragement. Where is the hammer?

24. Build a House of Cards

A challenge, no doubt, but an architect and construction mogul you could still be. Build your model skyscrapers into the attic and through the roof. If you are still invigorated by learning, you will find the metaphor littered with clues that all is temporary; all matter, form and function. With meaning inherent in every social and physical structure, the only question is: how deep are you willing to look?

25. Jump Out of a Plane

Some people like to jump out of perfectly good airplanes. Don't ask this author why; he's only recommending it because he had to come up with 555 Ways To Get a Kick Out of Retirement (and agreed with the people who decide such matters that closet daredevil-types may need a literal push).

26. Put The Rubber To The Road

Nearly everyone who grew up with winter is a wannabe hockey player or figure skater who dreamed of joining the *Ice Capades* or heavy-hitting NHL. But what if you grew up spending Christmas Day at the beach, or didn't have a TV? Get yourself down to the nearest sporting goods store and strap on some rubber rollers and take to the streets (or the driveway) like a road warrior. If you can't stop, do like all amateurs do: head for the boards.

27. Make A Hole-In-One

According to actuaries, the odds of an average golfer making a hole-in-one are 12,5000-to-1. On the other hand, a pro narrows the gap to 2,500-to-1. But don't let that discourage you, especially if the promotional alcohol, automobile and travel company prizes (not to mention bragging rights) are just too attractive.

28. Ski a Double Black Diamond Run

Bunny hill a little too tame for you? As a go-getter of the darkest of gemstone proportions (double black diamond) you get to decide whether gravity is friend or foe. What could be more thrilling (and chilling) than skiing vertically down the side of a mountain on nothing but ice and snow, at break-neck (pun intended) speed? The answer: the air is better up there, as is the view. But like any rush, it's temporary. So do it again.

29. Become a Real Estate Agent

Take everything you have learned in your 60+ years and put it to good use tricking people into buying livable boxes they don't like and/or can't afford. On the brighter side: you genuinely like connecting buyers and sellers and taking home a tidy commission for your efforts. All you need to rake it in is sufficient funding; a friendly smile; the gift of the gab; sales ability; a telephone and a car (interest in and knowledge of your local real estate market helps too).

30. Drink Good Wine

You can pick up a better bottle of plonk with just a few more quid than you currently spend, so dig into those deep pockets Ebenezer you miser and by some happiness (good wine is the closest you're ever going to get to permanent temporary bliss).

31. Watch Wimbledon in Person

Why should you never fall in love with a tennis player? To them, 'love' means nothing more than being tied (to their opponent). Joking side, is there anything more painful that watching tennis in England? If - god forbid - this ungodly combination is your cup of tea (available with milk at the concession stand, by the way) feel free to join your fellow tennis hooligans at the *All England Club* next year.

32. Go Wild At The World Cup

Soccer is the most popular game in the world (maybe because all it takes is having feet, which most people do; enough coordination to move said feet with a minimal dexterity; and access to *any* bouncy, round object. So if you love this sport, buy a ticket and go kick it where this sport outshines religion (and god doesn't even seem to mind).

33. Man-Up For The Stanley Cup Playoffs

Picture this: Your favorite team is playing their (and thus your) most-despised rivals. It's the 3rd period of the 7th game, the series is tied 3-3, and the scoreboard says 0-0. Where would you rather be when your team scores in overtime: getting flattened sweaty bikers in front of the flatscreen down at the local tavern, or roaring like an animal in the under-rated nose-bleed section?

34. Bungee Jump Naked

Who in their right mind would (pay to) jump off a bridge tied to nothing but a glorified elastic band? Apparently, if you go naked it's free. Still, many adrenaline-deprived people opt to spend a perfectly good afternoon in this death-defying pursuit of endorphins, discounting the age-old warning *"If your friends all jumped off a bridge, would you?"*

35. Wear Colored Contact Lenses

Not that eye color has anything to do with health, wealth and happiness (what everyone seems to be after in the end). But trying something new may just put a spring in your step or spice things up a little. And what better time to experiment than retirement? You care less about what other people think; you have time and money on your hands; and you are free to express your inner tiger / demon / flirt / angel / pussy cat.

35. Get a Job

Some people can't get a kick out of retirement. They miss being told what to do; when to do it; how to do it; what to wear while doing it; what to listen to (or not) while doing it; and how to think about what they are doing. If you miss being employed, there is no hope for retirement; you deserve all the kicks you can get. Go and get a job you workaholic.

37. Walk A Tight Rope

Have you ever wanted to join the circus, but the thought of flying through the air, juggling flaming chainsaws or swallowing swords was easier said than done? Fear not, undiscovered performance artist. Now that you've retired, you can fulfill your dreams in your own backyard. Buy a tight rope kit and be patient with yourself, because life is a balancing act.

38. Trapeze

If you can touch your toes and get back up without getting dizzy, losing your balance or pulling a muscle, Cirque du Soleil may be hiring (for support staff). Is it unrealistic at your age to believe you can leap from swing to swing like a monkey? Don't you dare fall victim to ageism; there are acrobatic training facilities across North America, and only 2 words: Do it.

39. Get a Monkey on Your Back

Watch your wallet and your watch when one of these tree branch-swingers lands on your shoulder and makes him / herself at home. Too bad they can't speak English; what tour guides they would be. When traveling in monkey country, don't be too liberal with the bananas, or you may never get rid of your new friend (if you could use another friend, these chimps come cheap: bananas cost pennies a bunch).

40. Do Jello Shots

There are fewer amusing ways to break the ice and get the party started than serving up the jello shots you stayed up all night making and clearing out your fridge to shelve. Yes, you can enjoy them on your own, but why? Any excuse for celebration is never far away; spiked, colored and sweetened gelatin 'shots' are a good enough reason for afternoon (or even before noon) debauchery any day of the year.

41. Witch For Water

Bend a couple of wire coat hangers and hold them so the pointy ends can freely swivel in your clenched fists. Now go for a walk and take note of your position when the wires start to move on their own. When this happens, you can call yourself a water witch (not too scary-sounding) and hire yourself out to well-drillers employed by daydreaming, city-fleeing, back-to-the-land wannabe homesteaders in search of a simple life.

42. Learn Stop Motion Animation

Move. Click. Move. Click. Move. Click. You get the idea. Set up a corner where your work won't be disturbed, and light it properly. Create or build or cut out or mold your actors, props and sets and steady your camera. Then move. Click. Move. Click. Move. Click until you're satisfied you've told your story. Now stitch together your stream of photos with some simple stop motion software and voilà!

43. Ski on Water

What were Jesus' followers smoking? It is understood that marijuana has increased in potency 20 times since at least the 1970's (if not since B.C.). Liquid hallucinations aside, you are encouraged to get friendly with someone who owns a speedboat, because you are never too old to be just like *The Miracle Man* himself.

44. Zip Through The Forest

"Heart-pounding thrills" and *"Fly through the forest."* At least that's what the brochures say ("defying gravity" is on the back flap). Letting your weight fling you across vast distances, far from the ground yet securely fastened by your harness to the steel cable strung between two trees, is why everyone is lining up to sign the disclaimer for the *"exhilarating treetop adventure"*.

45. Jump off a Cliff

If the high diving board has never been high enough (or the sensation of having your stomach jockey for position in your head with your brain doesn't even register in the bowels of your nervous system) then why not leap from a cliff with A) a small parachute (known as base jumping), or B) nothing but water beneath you? Either way, you will be surrounded by other 'crazies' so at least you won't die alone.

46. Spend a Night in a Teepee

With nothing more than an ornate rustic tent between you and the scream-muffling boonies, sleeping in a circle with complete strangers and/or your nearest and dearest is the closest you're going to get to dancing with wolves. But combine a night in a teepee with a sauna-like sweat lodge experience, and you may just up and legally change your name to *Two Dogs Mating*.

47. Colonize Mars

You might have to sacrifice your life for the greater good, but if the other 545 ways to get a kick out of retirement are leaving you cold, what else are you going to do? Scientists and futurists alike believe Mars could be the next earth, so if you have 10 billion dollars in your pocket (Elon Musk's estimate) and yet-to-be-developed technology sitting in your basement, perhaps you could lead the first mission to the red planet.

48. Sing Karaoke

You don't have to be Celine Dion or Pavarotti to sing karaoke. Bribe a few friends to join you for a night out (if they are initially reluctant, keep your destination a secret and surprise them when you bust out a timeless hit from *The King of Pop*, or raunchy classic rock anthem that gets everyone in the dimly-lit club singing backup). Note: as in all things, never take yourself too seriously.

49. Stomp on Grapes

You can't buy happiness, but you can buy wine (and that's kind of the same thing). When 7.5 million hectares of earth have been devoted to growing grapes, you don't have to travel far if you dream of drowning your feet (and later your sorrows) in the fermented varietals you so like to drink. You will be supplied with booties instead of dancing shoes, so that foot fungus and those hang-nails are non-issues. Cheers!

50. Grow Lavender

If you have trouble sleeping, lavender will summon the Sandman. When distilled into essential oil, this herb is the most versatile; it smells nice; it's easy to grow; you can eat it; and it's beautiful (if you like the color purple). Favored the world-over for its healing and therapeutic effects, your skin will love the lavender you lavish on it, for some say it's the only essential oil you will ever need.

51. Play Laser Tag

Zap! Bleep! Duck! Shoot! Admittedly, your natural environment is devoid of strobe lights and florescent glow stick-lined alcoves, so hopefully you can defend yourself if you didn't enlist the help of a teenager or two to 'cover you' as you creep down the illuminated hallway, futuristic pistol poised for a perfect shot. The best part is that beams of light are painless (in comparison to being pelted with a paintball at point-blank range).

52. Work with Stained Glass

Elizabeth Kubler-Ross says *"People are like stained-glass windows. They sparkle when the sun is out, but when it gets dark, their true beauty can only be seen if there is a light from within."* Like many artists, options are limited only by one's imagination. So what do you see when you shine a light on your creative soul?

53. Buy a Boat

The biggest threat to boaters is not what BOAT stands for (Bring Out Another Thousand). The greatest danger looming under the surface is "Foot-itis". Easy to spot, this affliction is most commonly interpreted as the desire for more overall footage. Beware: outbreaks happen while reading boating magazines, attending boat shows, or participating in fishing derbies. But once contracted, there is a cure: take your friends and family out on the water as often as possible.

54. Sail Across The Ocean

If you can't see the horizon due to a particularly large swell, your compass and GPS will assure you it exists. If other people can cross enormous bodies of water in vessels ranging from dinghies to freighters, you can bob the ocean blue too. Just tether yourself to the mast like you were a baby on reins.

55. Pimp Your Ride

Ever wash your car / truck / bike, and then upon admiring your handy work, have the urge to upgrade? Before you go trading in your jalopy for a low-rider, do what the kids do: pimp your ride. Love has no price, so if you dote on the machine under your butt or between your legs, learn the tricks of the trade and/or spend the bucks to spiff it up (fuzzy dice optional).

56. Pan for Gold

The gold rush was the largest mass migration in US history, attracting immigrants from around the world (though you may know that more fortunes were made by the merchants who sold picks and shovels to the nugget-hungry miners). Nowadays, with a tin pan, a pound of patience, and a fleck of luck, you can strike it rich in any river or stream in the world.

57. Eat Fruit From a Tree

Apart from growing a garden and harvesting your own fresh veggies (or scaling a coconut palm like a monkey) if you have never picked an apple, pear or pomegranate from a tree and gobbled it up on the spot, give into temptation. There is a reason Adam and Eve got in so much trouble (relax: you will never wreck things like they did).

58. Play Frisbee Golf

Dogs aren't the only ones having a great time chasing flying plastic discs. According to the *Professional Disc Golf Association*, the object of this skillful game is to *"traverse a course from beginning to end in the fewest number of throws of your disc."* Fun and challenging, frisbee golf is played in 40 countries (which means there is probably a course nearby).

Get out of the house!

59. Go Skating on an Outdoor Rink

The capital of Canada boasts the longest outdoor skating rink in the world. Folks even commute to-and-from work on the frozen canal. Families north of the frostbitten 60th Parallel flood their backyards and play ice hockey all winter, joined by peeps of all ages. What is the point? It's never too late to summon your inner child (or grow icicles on your eyebrows).

60. Ride in an Amphibious Vehicle

Cars can't fly (yet) but they can swim, take you fishing, or get you safely across the lake when the bridge is washed out (you never know when that will happen). Most popular during the 1960's, floating road-worthy vehicles are currently not too sought after, which would make owning and/or riding in one a unique experience (and even more expensive).

61. Swim Across a Lake

Looks like you could make it, right? Rest assured, it's further than it seems (just ask the peeps who call themselves long distance swimmers). Let's be honest: if you haven't already swam across a lake, it's not likely overflowing from your bucket list. In this case, swimming from one end of the hot tub to the other may be enough of an accomplishment at your age.

62. Do The Splits

Just because a 3-year-old can do the splits doesn't mean you can (you may be decades from stretching your body like that). But that doesn't mean it's impossible. If spreading your legs for fitness is your way of staying lean and limber, don't push yourself more than usual, because you will probably need your muscles to get out of bed tomorrow morning.

63. See How Low You Can Go

If you become a limbo champion, don't walk into a bar... or your may lose your title. Originating on the island of Trinidad and popularized by Julia Edwards and Chubby Checker, dancing the limbo involves shimmying your body underneath the bar (as opposed to the high jump - where as a participant you are expected to jump over it). Some people raise the bar. Others lower it.

64. Hula Hoop for 5 Minutes

In the dark comedy *The Hudsucker Proxy,* Tim Robbins' bumbling mailroom employee character invents the hula hoop (which turns out to be a massive success for his company) yet few grasp the concept at first (hence the entertainment). Such a delightful diversion, hula-hooping is an easy exercise you can do in your living room (you are allowed to work your way up to the 5-minute mark).

65. Play Tennis

Played (and watched) by millions of people worldwide, the first tennis club was established in 1872 in Birmingham, England (and ever since that glorious day, both singles and doubles have been swatting balls back and forth trying to get one over on a woman standing in the middle of the court named Annette).

66. Play Golf

How do you know you're never too old to play golf? If you ever need a cane, just use your putter! There are but 3 steps to the game: Use a club - to hit a ball - into a hole. If you are fanatical about this sport, your passion (read: obsession) is perfectly normal, so even if you are only starting out, pretend your father is there in spirit to criticize your swing (you probably already hear his voice in your head).

67. Do a Somersault

Ever long for the wonder you experienced in childhood? Somersaults don't cost a dime (unless you don't have medical insurance, in which case, chiropractors aren't cheap). But barring spinal disaster, you will make it through relatively unscathed (unless good hair days are head-and-shoulders more important to you). When was the last time you rolled over (head first) for no reason at all?

68. Stand On Your Hands

Feeling a little stagnant? Want to improve your circulation? Handstands will get your blood flowing again. If extreme acrobatic poses are a little foreign to you (and you have zero desire to accomplish such a strenuous feat) then begin with a few simple stretches. Worried about becoming flat-footed? Walk upside down and get flat palms instead.

69. Line Dance The Night Away

Yes, you may (will) look silly at first (if you believe the haters) but like many public displays of enjoyment, stepping onto the dance floor, learning a move or two, and letting your hair down is all you will ever need to do the next time you want to get down get down.

70. Swim Like a Fish

Would you like to be more confident in the water? Swimming lessons are affordable, effective and safe (and you might even make some friends). Even olympic athletes started splashing around the shallow end as grubby guppies and tiny tadpoles, so strap on some sexy goggles, keep the h2o out of your nasal passage with a clothes pin (if you're on a budget), don a sporty (or leopard-spotted) hair net to complete the ensemble, and make for the deep end.

71. Go Fishing

Seafood is good for you (free seafood is even better). Support aquaculture and marine conservation efforts. Relieve stress. Bond with your buddies / colleagues / clients / kids. Get outside and enjoy some fresh air. Experience the thrill of the catch. Shamelessly drink beer before noon. Do you need further convincing?

72. Go Hunting

People have been hunting and gathering for longer than they have been shopping at Walmart. Even though fewer folks are trudging out into the bush armed with various weaponry and outfitted in the latest camouflage, hunting is the most ethical (and affordable) way to source free-range red meat (you might have to get your hands dirty). The only question is: where does your T-bone steak come from?

73. Stretch Yourself Out

According to *The American Osteopathic Association*, the physical benefits of yoga are numerous. Yoga (gently) increases your flexibility, muscle strength and tone; improves your cardiovascular / respiratory system (so you can breathe easier), and balances your metabolism (which can help you lose weight). Where is the next drop-in class?

74. Ride a Ferris Wheel

Ever since George Washington Gale Ferris Jr. unveiled the ferris wheel at the Columbian Expo in Chicago in 1893, his spinning metal contraption with bucket seats has prevented young lovers from getting from first to second base with their dates. But if you never made it to lover's lane, not to worry: the ride of lost lunches and broken hearts is coming soon to a town near you.

75. Watch People Fight

...at a live boxing match (not beside an empty swimming pool in your backyard surrounded with shirtless drunks high on crack cocaine). Nowadays, there are mixed-martial art bouts (where nearly everything goes) but if you're more of a purist, stick with the recognized, state-sanctioned Olympic fights, where the gloves never come off. If you are a fan of Mike Tyson, you may like to know that his computer has two bites and no memory.

76. Set a 1000 Piece Puzzle

The puzzles at the thrift store not stirring your imagination? Why not turn your favorite travel photo into a puzzle? You get to choose how many pieces: 4 / 8 / 12 / 50 / 100 / 500 / 1000 (depending on how much time you have for this peaceful skill-testing pursuit). The secret is to start with the outside edge and forget all about time.

77. Ride a Go-Kart

You may or may not get pole position (it depends on who you go with). If not, don't pout like it's your birthday (you must feign complacency, for when they least expect it, you will sneak by them on the 3rd turn and cruise over the finish line, having earned the right to gloat as you complete your victory lap). Indoors or out, push the pedal to the carbon-fiber floor.

78. Play Twister

Naked or not, playing *Twister* has nothing to do with tornadoes (such an activity is best left to professionals). The game that was inducted into the Toy Hall of Fame that you *can* play at home (if you can still bend and twist and get up afterwards) all starts with a spin of the dial (after which fate takes over and dictates what you do next). Yes, you *could* play alone, but that's no fun.

79. Throw a Boomerang

Aborigines in the Australian outback have used boomerangs to clunk kangaroos on the head since they sang everything into existence eons ago (while unearthed European models date back to the Stone Age, when it is believed these primal engineers stumbled upon the return trip by accident). Available anywhere frisbees are sold.

80. Repel from a Rock Wall

As long as you don't buy your caribiner clips from the dollar store, you may live to climb another mountain (but don't rule it out; you just may meet a fellow repeller in the dried fruit and nut section of said discount warehouse). But are rock climbers all fruits and nuts? That is another book. If you want to play it safe, hitch your wagon to one of these 'people' if you want to make it home in once piece without cracking your shell (or theirs).

81. Snorkel Through a Coral Reef

If you can swim, you can snorkel. All you need is a mask, a snorkel (duh) and some fins (rent them before you go and buy a set, in case it turns out not to turn your crank). You can go snorkeling anywhere in the world, though in some locales you may want to slip into a zebra-striped wet suit (which has the dual advantage of keeping you warm while also making you invisible to sharks).

82. Walk Across a Suspension Bridge

Rule #1. Don't let a trouble-maker tag along. Said tricksters can quickly push you to the brink of fright from which you may not quickly recover. There are few terrifying moments in one's life more-easily manifested than swinging more-than-feels-comfortable way too far from the bottom of a ravine. The best advice is (and has always been) don't look down.

83. Start or Stop Wearing Make Up

Understandably, if you have worn make up your whole life, there is little chance you will stop now. But maybe you have outgrown the façade and wish to let your natural beauty shine through. On the other hand, if you have never worn make up, would you start now? Maybe a makeover is overdue (as is cross-dressing, if this is your thing).

84. Win an Arm Wrestling Competition

The World Armwrestling Federation claims that technique and overall arm strength are the deciding factors in a win against an opponent. Practice on your grandkids; they will love the challenge and attention (and may be well-matched, depending on your abilities). Don't forget (or be discouraged): Chuck Norris regularly wins with both of his arms tied behind his back.

85. Do a Flip on a Trampoline

The worst than can happen is you fall and break your neck. So get one with a net (so the worse than can happen is you have to wallow in your shame a little longer after failing to nail a perfect triple-axel in mid-air in front of the spectators). Screw the judges if they don't give you unanimous 10's because you landed on your bum; they have to go back to school or work (whereas you can spend the next 10 or 20 years perfecting your technique).

86. Ride a Bucking Bronco

Start at the country and western saloon in the closest place resembling Dodge City in your hovel, city, town, village or metropolis. Climb onto that mechanical bull, drop a coin in the slot, and hang on for dear life. Choose the beginner setting so you can get saddle-sore well before the circus comes to town and your best friend becomes the rodeo clown.

87. Throw a Javelin

There are 3 ways to grip the pole correctly: the American grip; the Finnish grip and the V Grip (so make sure you are off to a good start before launching the spear into the air). Hold it near your head, pick a target, take a run at it and let it go. Where do you get your hands on a javelin? If there isn't a track and field store nearby, see if you can find some lawn darts at a garage sale (they were banned in 1988).

88. Be a Zoo Keeper for a Day

Feeding, breeding and cleaning up after your favorite animals can be a messy good time in a safe and protected enclosure surrounded with professional (armed) beast handlers. But don't ask this author how to zoo keep for a day; getting a kick out of your retirement is up to you. Regardless of how you go about it, Zoo Keeper will look great in the volunteer section of your resume (if you ever need one again).

89. Ride a Water Slide

You are never too old to go feet-first on a carpet of running water down a dark tunnel during the day (or in broad, sunny daylight) accompanied by the shrieks and screams of kids of all ages. If you don't mind getting wet (and especially if you have never slipped and slid around on slides as high as 3-story buildings) muster the crew for some family-friendly summer fun and go head first.

90. Go Camping

Fear not the lions, tigers, bears, mosquitos, noisy generators and interrupted sleep. The best parts of camping are the fresh air; being mesmerized by the flames of a nightly campfire; the s'mores; cold beer from the cooler; and the best part: forgetting the real world even exists. Ah, the great outdoors. Ah, backyards.

91. Become a Scientologist

Nicole Kidman was the best thing to happen to Tom Cruise (though he chose to give his love - and money - to a bankrupt writer). Marketed as the *Study of Truth*, this 21st Century religion will suck you dry to the tune of $50,000 (just to get up to speed). So if you are bored, lost, rich, and looking for meaning, catch a one-way to the Celebrity Center in Los Angeles.

92. Get Your Palms Read

What do the hills, valleys, plateaus and plains on your palms say about your past, present and future? Would an interpretation of such mundane (yet possibly ancient) mysteries from a sagely seer bring you comfort or peace? Such guidance will only serve you in the moment, as you (realistically) have other matters to attend to (which is why the fine print: *"For entertainment purposes only"* absolves the psychic of all responsibility).

93. Learn To Astral Travel

Otherwise known as astral projection, voluntarily leaving your physical body via soul or spirit can feel like an acid trip to the un-initiated. If you are not deterred, put yourself into a state of relaxation via deep breathing or your favorite meditation before visualizing your soul / spirit leaving your body. You don't need a passport, but please buy a return ticket.

94. Study Astrology

Your body is made up of roughly 60% water, so could the moon (and other celestial bodies in your gravity-controlled solar system) effect your biology? While some astrologers claim psychic powers and intuition, others employ mathematics and mix symbology, geometry and psychology into their counseling practices. Whether you believe the woo-woo or not, the art and science of the stars has fascinated humankind for centuries.

95. Learn Numerology

According to numerology, everything noun in existence has a corresponding numerical value (or vibration). Each number (1 through 9) represents a different aspect of the human experience. So just like Alice, if you dare dive down the rabbit hole (and you are intuitive and/or imaginative) tread lightly, or you will never count to 10 the same way again.

96. Start a New Religion

Do your daily beliefs and/or practices counter those of most people? The more passionate and charismatic you are about your views and ideas, the better chance you have of getting everyone to drink your colorful concoction. It's simple, really: Write a book; get it read; build a church; get some attention; recruit some lost sheep willing to sign over everything they own to the 'higher good' and you are in business.

97. Participate in a Seance

Abraham Lincoln's wife used to host these other-worldly 'sittings' in the White House. Back then it was all smoke and mirrors, though who knows if or what spirits lurk in our midst (and/or if we can communicate with them). Are you curious? Hunt down an experienced medium and ask your ancestors where they buried your inheritance. Wouldn't you like to know?

98. Read the Bible

To most sensible non-religious people, the Bible is just another book (albeit the record-holder for number of copies in print). If there isn't one on your bedside table (and your parents didn't read it to you before bed every night) arm yourself with the fictionalized facts before you playfully debate the proselytizers on the street corner.

99. Become a Whirling Dervish

Not just another Turkish Muslim tourist attraction, the goal of this ecstatic ceremonial dance is a form of meditation wherein Sufi mystics aim to reach enlightenment. Vetted by Rumi (the best-selling poet in the USA) would suggest there must be something to it, no?

100. Renounce Everything

This is not for the faint-of-heart, fellow retiree. Chances are, you are still surrounded with old photos, nicknacks and used twist ties of various sizes (and are more than happy that things stay as they are, thank-you-very-much). In addition, you would likely only ever consider this rash lifestyle change as a symbol of your adherence to religious doctrine. But when there are pros and cons to everything, have you ever wondered: what do they know that I don't?

101. Embrace The F Word

"Fear will set you free / Skip the pharmacy" begins one of the first poems yours truly ever penned. When some people experience the F word (fear) they can fall into the trap of taking expensive, habit-forming, mind-numbing drugs. How about this instead: When fear appears out of nowhere (as it often does) the bigger bear hug you give it, the bigger the kick out of retirement you will get. Guaranteed.

102. Dance in the Rain

Dance partner or not, how important is celebrating your golden years? Is dancing in the rain simply the romantic notion of dreamers? Absolutely. Is it also a light-hearted (albeit risqué) way to entertain yourself? Absolutely. You wear clothes all day, so why not fling off not only your outer layer, but also your unmentionables? 5 fewer items of clothing equals 5 times more fun.

103. Bathe in Milk

According to history, both Cleopatra and Queen Liz the first rejoiced in the beautifying benefits of milk baths. Apparently, lactic acid dissolves dead skin cells, so the next time it's time to exfoliate, take a dip in a whole lotta milk to soften your skin before scrubbing away said skin cells with your favorite loofa and soothe your bones in the naturally-fortified liquid of life.

104. Make a Soundtrack of Your Life

What were your favorite songs as a teenager? And what was the first song you ever learned the lyrics to? Music had such an otherworldly impact on your impressionable mind when you were young that you can still recall how you felt and where you were, whenever you hear a certain song (no matter how long ago it was). Turn on the radio, turn up the volume and turn back time. Make a soundtrack to your life.

105. Surround Yourself with Good People

Did you know you are the average of the 5 people you spend the most time with? This goes for finances; your emotional well-being; and social status. Who doesn't want to be financially, emotionally and socially happy and healthy? You won't regret the things you did; you will regret the things you didn't do.

106. Get Into Shape

It's never too late to get into shape (especially if you have been putting it off your entire life). How many times have you thought about getting fit, or even bought yourself a gym membership? Fewer retirement-age pursuits will benefit you more than getting into shape (but you know that already). Nothing you do will make you feel better about yourself than getting into shape. Forget retirement; this is your last chance to get a (high) kick out of life.

107. Read a Self Improvement Book

No matter your personality-type, there is a guru out there to kick you in the pants and/or hold your hand on your way to healthier relationships; more resources; and less stress and suffering than you currently experience. At the very least, you will learn the moral of the story G.I. Joe aimed to teach at the end of each episode: *"Knowing is half the battle."*

108. Shower Under a Waterfall

While dancing in the rain is a frivolous pursuit, showering under a waterfall has practical benefits. You just stand there (bathing suit or not) and let the aquatic pressure pound your sore shoulders into putty (regardless of how much weight the world has thrust upon them). Cheaper than a massage (and no water bill to worry about) a waterfall will wash your retirement worries away (until you start sweating again).

109. Forgive Someone

Who have you disowned, neglected or written-off? Wouldn't now be a good time to reconcile your differences and make peace with the past? You have a choice: you can be right, or you can be kind. What have you got to lose? Why suffer any longer? Don't you miss the connection / love / joy / fun you shared? Pick up the phone.

110. Discover Your Life's Purpose

What were you born to do? Do you even know? It's never too late to find meaning and joy in your life via a creative / inspirational / passionate pursuit. People have received degrees; written books; climbed mountains; saved endangered species; rocked the Casbah; and exchanged marriage vows well into their later years. Belief is the only barrier to achieving the impossible. How else are you going to get a kick out retirement?

1:1-1. Toot In Church

To all the self-righteous, holier-than-thou sanctimonious goody-goodies, tooting in church is blasphemous (which is why this way to get a kick out of retirement is perfect for the pious). Treat yourself to a hearty bean casserole and take the organic orchestra to midnight mass. The one who laughs first buys breakfast (go for Mexican).

112. Fast

Like meditating, fasting on nothing / water / fruit juice / consommé for any length of time will most likely try your last ounce of liquid (or solid) patience and push you to the limits of willpower. It's not your fault; you grew up eating 3 meals a day. Fast only if you have ever considered giving your digestion a rest (there is endless information available to guide you; find something that resonates).

113. Create an App

The future is here, grandpa. If for any reason you know your way around a computer and have always fancied being a programmer, there has never been a better time. Even *Google* offers simple app building software that anyone with a head on their shoulders; a little patience; and a degree of motivation can use to create something useful.

114. Conquer an Addiction Cold Turkey Style

There is a reason people do things the old-school way. If you have been wresting with an addiction, why not triumph over your achilles heel that sabotages you in more ways than one? Like any attempt at 'changing your life' this is no different (you will do what is most important to you). How badly do you want to change? You can teach an old dog new tricks. Commit.

115. Get Out of Debt

It's easier to get in than out, but that doesn't mean you should drown yourself in the well just because climbing out would take some effort. You can conquer the debt monster. Like ending an addiction cold turkey-style, freezing your credit card in a block of ice will force you to melt before you attempt to fulfill another need with money (and the stuff it can buy) which never seems to work.

116. Go Blonde

Blondes likely have more fun, but brunettes wouldn't know (nor would the redheads or the raven-haired among us). The point is: you are not getting any younger. So why not see for yourself if blondes have more fun? A bottle of peroxide will only set you back a few bucks.
On the other hand, you could always shave your head and buy a wig.

117. Ride A Ski-Dog

The best-selling motorized brand of snow sled was originally named *ski-dog*, though thanks to a typo, turned out to be ski-doo. In the event you have to get from A to B in winter (and there are no roads between A and B) then you probably already own one. Or maybe you have never even seen snow (in which case, disregard everything you just read).

118. Zip Around on a Jet Ski

Like to go fast? Like to get wet? Like to annoy innocent bystanders involved in peacetime non-motorized water sports? Jet skiing might be right for you (ask your doctor). If you have yet to zip across the water *not* tied to a speed boat, or have always thought how much fun all those people must be having, jet ski club membership comes cheap; you can rent these aquatic pocket rockets by the hour.

119. Get a Full Body Massage

Whether or you opt for the 'happy ending' or not, nothing beats calming (or invigorating) touch. Worth its wait in gold, a full body massage will rid your body, blood stream and mind of any toxins (emotional, physical or otherwise) invading the sacred space you call your body. Plaguing negativity swept away, you will feel as relaxed as a wet noodle, so if your masseuse starts boiling water, run!

120. Get Acupuncture

Does acupuncture relieve swelling, enhance blood flow and encourage healing? Or are victims (read: patients) simply subjecting themselves to voluntary torture? The answer is up to you; only you know whether needles are friend or foe. As with choosing anything, follow your gut (unless your gut is has been stuck like a pig, and that tingling feeling is hurting more than it seems to be helping).

121. Take a Cooking Class

The more time and energy you invest in preparing your own food, the more your food will nourish and delight you. If you don't know the difference between an oven and a microwave, sign up for a cooking class through a local kitchen store or community college (unless you have always wanted to go to cooking school). Fun, friendly, informative and delicious, these educational events are also great gifts for the passionate cook or baker in your life.

122. Host a Themed Dinner Party

Decorate the house, plan a menu, go shopping, get dressed up and cook for days. Your dinner party guests will appreciate the effort. Or if you like murder mysteries, get your friends or family together for a night you will all remember, for your foray into foodie festivities will be something you all savor for years.

123. Make Pasta from Scratch

If you don't like pasta, you have never made it from scratch. Al dente requires seconds (not minutes). And you only need 3 ingredients: flour, eggs and water. Knead it all into a ball, roll it out, cut it and dry it on a floured hanger. Now before adding the pasta to the rolling boil, be sure to follow this author's cooking school instructor's advice: *"the water should be saltier than the sea."*

124. Brew Your Own Hooch

Here are 5 good reasons to make your own moonshine (or beer, wine, cider, mead). #1. It tastes good. #2. It gets you drunk. #3. If you don't have any friends, most people can be bribed with liquor. #4. If you buy booze from the store, you will save money by making your own. #5. You can be creative. Already dreaming up more reasons to brew your own hooch? You don't need any more convincing.

125. Host a Cocktail Party

Besides satisfying your original desires upon arriving at the liquor store, if collecting the cocktail recipe books doesn't become a hobby in itself, expanding your horizons (and liquor cabinet) with fancy tipple in ever fancier bottles will get you sauced on mixology. A splash of invitations, and handful of friends, a dash or two of some nummy nosh and you got yourself a cocktail party.

126. Bake a Pie

Blackberry; blueberry; apple; peach; cherry; rhubarb; raspberry; boysenberry; lemon chiffon; pumpkin chiffon; banana cream; chocolate cream; chocolate tofu cream; coconut cream; butterscotch; raisin; pecan; sugar; shepherd's; pork; chicken pot; turkey; bacon and egg; beef; cashew; custard; seal flipper. You get the picture; you can buy the pastry at the grocery store in the frozen aisle.

127. Make Your Own Pizza

While doing hard time in 3 pizza shops, this author concocted timeless hits like pesto / broccoli / cauliflower and smoked salmon / cream cheese / red onion / capers. Use quality ingredients, stoke the coals (the hotter the oven, the better) and don't burn your pie.

128. Create a Family Recipe Book

A young cook once wondered why her mother cut the ends off the roast before putting it in the pan. So she asked her. She said she didn't know; she had always done it that way. So they got grandma on the phone and grandma said the same thing. So they called great-grandma and she replied: because it wouldn't fit in the pan! Capture the stories behind your family's favorite recipes (unless Aunt Jemima and Uncle Ben whip up all your meals) so you can course-correct along the way. But only if you believe in evolution.

129. Hack Open a Coconut

In every tropical country in the world, locals wait to hack open their coconuts in exchange for your money. And they make it look so easy. So if upon acclimatizing to your new-found paradise (it takes at least 14 days to unwind) you find yourself thinking *I could do that*, ask a tourist-friendly local and his trusty machete for a lesson.

130. Build a Gingerbread House

There are few holiday baking undertakings more magical to a young (or young-at-heart) baker than baking, building and decorating a Gingerbread House. Of course, it all starts with a visit to the candy aisle at the bulk store. But even if you opt for a pre-fab kit, the magic is still in the... er, box. So there is only one question you must ask yourself: are you a contractor or an owner-builder?

131. Create a Signature Drink

Believe it or not, this author had a handful of friends growing up. At one such shindig where they had gathered sans-parents, 'paralyzers' were all the rage, so just to be different, this writer concocted the following: 1 part tequila, 1 part vodka, 2 parts orange juice, 2 parts 7-up, and called it *The Ollie-Izer*. What will *your* signature drink pay tribute to? And what will you call it?

132. Eat Escargot

In case you were wondering whether escargot gets any press, May 24th has been deemed *National Escargot Day* in the United States. If you haven't tried them (and are at all curious what all the fuss is about) you will soon know whether you will be devoting this often pleasant pre-summer day giving alms to the slippery little suckers or not.

133. Toast Marshmallows on a Stick

The time-honored camping ritual of finding - and carving a tip on - the perfect stick, reaching into the sticky, puffy bag, and toasting your prized morsel of congealed, spun sugar into the consistency of molten lava cannot be properly explained in words. If you have forgotten the simple culinary delights possible around a roaring (or coal furnace) campfire, that's what grandkids are for.

134. Make Homemade Potato Chips

If you are what you eat, who wouldn't want to be a potato chip? Consider the humble spud; the engineering of a vegetable peeler; what genius invented deep frying (or peanut oil for that matter); and how primal an endeavor harvesting salt from the earth (or sea) can be. Divide this all by 4 ingredients and the answer is junk food heaven. There is nothing like it.

135. Find a Truffle Mushroom

Just so you know: you can't buy a Truffle pig on *Amazon*, or rent one like a car on *Expedia*, so don't even try. But you don't need a trained pig to fetch the most expensive single food ingredient in the world; you can train your dog to sniff them out for you. Bury one in a sock and train them to play hide-and-seek with the obvious command *"Find the truffle!"* They will love it.

136. Become a Vegetarian / Vegan

How do know someone is a vegan? Don't worry, they will tell you. Both vegetarians and vegans s(pr)out the benefits of their food choices for good reason. Vegetarians tend to live longer than carnivores (yet omnivores have way more fun in both the kitchen and around the dinner table). But seriously, whether your motivations be spiritual or based on well-being, consider food your medicine.

137. Make Homemade Jam

Fruit was made to be jam, right? How else were we supposed to enjoy the sweet harvest throughout the year? Pick or buy (or pay to pick) your favorite fruit and invest in some canning supplies (they are reusable). Then find a recipe or an experienced friend and make a day out of it. What a great gift for the loved ones in your life.

138. Cook a Turkey

There are as many ways to cook a turkey as there are wannabe chefs, but there are a few basics. Buy a local bird, if possible. Brine or smoke him or her for exceptional flavor. Make your own stuffing (that's a book on its own). Now cook your gobbler based on its weight. And make soup and sandwiches with the left overs. Or just say *"to hell with it all"* and deep-fry it in corn oil until it's golden brown, crispy and beyond delicious.

139. Make Sangria

After water, juice, tea, coffee, and various other alcoholic drinks, what is left? Wine punch. After a few hundred milliliters have passed your lips, nothing else matters except a siesta in the shade. Countries, cultures and companies have all been built on grapes and oranges, so buy your ticket to a Spanish-speaking country and viva happy hour!

140. Eat Poutine in Québec

If you ever mention to a foodie that you have visited (or will be visiting) the French-speaking province of Canada, it won't be long before you are asked if you have tried poutine. A gooey trough of french fries, gravy and cheese curds (you can add chili, foie gras, fried onions, pickled herring, pulled pork... you get the idea), poutine is a cultural experience.

141. Spike a Watermelon

Cut some 'corks' out of a watermelon and scoop out just a spoonful. Invert a few 12oz bottles of your favorite booze into the holes and put it in the fridge for 3 days. The watermelon will soak up any amount of liquid you add, so all you have to worry about is having enough cushions for everyone to pass out on in your living room.

142. Host an Ice Cream Sundae Party

Your shopping list will depend on your guest list, but you can't go wrong by supplying the basics (chocolate, vanilla and strawberry ice cream) and asking everyone to pitch in potluck-style and bring their favorite toppings. The saying *"the more, the merrier"* applies to both guests and toppings, so don't be shy. And if you are a grumpy old goat, be careful: This is a recipe for fun.

143. Eat a Deep-Fried Mars Bar

At some point in recent Scottish history, a clever lad or lass thought to dip one of the finest candy bars in simple fish batter, deep-fry it, and eat it. You have not lived until you have partaken, so when you do, don't be surprised if you black out and wake up in heaven.

144. Make Your Own Candy

What confection had you contemplating the logistics of trading your own brother or sister for a lifetime supply of your favorite treat as a child? Now that you have (hopefully) mended burned bridges, what treats would *they* love as a thoughtful gift on their next birthday? Candy-making defies the rules of food, so explore, experiment and enchant your inner child with the sinfully sweet or ticklishly-sour sugar-laden goodies you and your loved ones miss most.

145. Visit Your Childhood Home

If you have positive memories of your early years, this is a no-brainer. Otherwise, skip ahead (this book is about enjoying yourself; not opening closets chock-full of skeletons). Sauntering down memory lane and reflecting on our past often brings understanding, resolution and healing (but only if you can be patient with yourself, and appreciate and respect such a potentially profound experience).

146. Write Your Obituary

What would you say about yourself? What would others say? What would your mother say? What would your father say? What would your best friend say? How do you want to be remembered? What are you most proud of? Who did you admire? How did you emulate them? You could go on forever, obviously, but you get the idea. Everything comes to an end, so have fun.

147. Reconnect with Childhood Friends

Whether you loathe or love social media and the instant interconnection that seems to span space and time, you may also fear virtually bumping into high school bullies and slighted exes (though love reconnecting with kindred spirits who spontaneously flit into and out of your life in what now seem like comet-like moments). Who would you like to cross paths with or meet again?

148. Make a Wish on Dandelion Fluff

Not genie, nor four-leaf clover, nor fairy godmother, nor shooting star, nor shopping mall wishing well has the power to grant your wish like dandelion fluff. Whether you are 3 or 93, you have always wished this to be true (so don't let anyone fool you into believing otherwise). Especially now. What have you got to lose?

149. Laugh Until You Cry

This doesn't happen enough, for some reason. So from now on, when it does, ensure it happens again (before enough time goes by that you forget how much fun you had). When was the last time you couldn't breathe because something or someone was so funny it / they took your breath away? In retirement, nothing matters more than your pleasure, appreciation and enjoyment of your life.

150. Patent an Invention

Stay away from the sharks circling wannabe inventors waiting to 'cash in' on unsuspecting swimmers with good ideas (unless you see yourself pitching your stuff on Shark Tank or Dragon's Den). Instead, go straight to the feds (they hold all the cards anyway). With a lot of patience, persistence and perspective, you can patent your own invention so your heirs can reap the rewards long after you're gone.

151. Sculpt a Statue

Clay is a good start. Stone, if you know what you're doing. Steel if you appreciate the aesthetic. Simple earth works too. It's never too late to create. If you feel driven to emulate (or are inspired by) the works of great architects / masons / sculptors, you could take a course at your local art college. Trial-by-error works too (giving yourself the permission and freedom to fumble is liberating).

152. Catch Fireflies in a Jar

Poke holes in the lid of a glass jar and toss in some wet paper towel to keep the air humid. Then sneak up on them with a net and voila! You will find them anywhere hot and humid, near standing water (just like mosquitoes). But despite more than 2,000 species of light bugs, only a few emit what is known as *"the most efficient light source in the world."*

153. Send a Message in a Bottle

Just like shipwrecked sailors of yore couldn't be sure their message reached the intended recipient, if you lob one of these into the sea, don't expect a reply any time soon. But if you rather appreciate the romanticism of a humble manifesto succumbing to the mercy of the high seas, set sail. Just let go of any attachment to who reads your long-lost love note... or when... it could be a while.

154. Watch a Meteor Shower

Meteors are dancing across the sky all year round. Consult the American Meteor Society (founded in 1911) for dates and locations, then get to a low-light area (ideally during or following a New Moon), set up your telescope (if you have one) and enjoy the show. Pack a picnic, a blanket, and a cuddle partner for maximum enjoyment.

155. Rope Swing into a Lake

You are never too old to climb up a tree, grab a rope and cowabunga into a lake in the summer time. Regardless of whether you let the braver lab-rat daredevils test the waters first, wait to let go of the rope until you are clear of the shore and debris below.

156. Catch a Snowflake on Your Tongue

When was the last time you tasted a cool, acid-rain-flavored snowflake on your tongue, only to return to the endless buffet for more? Remember what Lucy from the *Charlie Brown Christmas* holiday special declared: *"I never eat December snowflakes. I always wait until January or February,"* to which Linus wisely replied *"They sure look ripe to me."* Whether your nose is in the air like Lucy, or you let your blanket defenses down like her little brother, there is nothing like a fresh 'homemade' snowflake melting on the tip of your tongue.

157. Build a Snowman

The inuit (eskimo) have 50 words for snow, so if conditions are right, get the snowballs rolling and play Dr. Frankenstein for an afternoon. As long as you can keep the catchy seasonal tune *Frosty The Snowman* from infiltrating your headspace, you might actually enjoy playing in the snow.

158. Make a Snow Angel

If you've come this far, you might as well go all the way: as long as you have arms and legs and there is snow on the ground (avoid the yellow stuff), you can decorate any square meter of ground with your unique creative contribution (the trick is getting back on your feet without destroying your frosty work of art when you're done). But hey, when your canvas is endless, you could just as easily leave your trademarked wing span all over Winter Town.

159. Name a Star

Now only $19.95. Call now and get a framed certificate for free. Hurry, this offer won't last. Sidestep all the promotional hype and find the real thing; usually an *International Star Registry* (or something to that cosmic effect). If you ever kicked yourself for not getting into real estate earlier (who hasn't) forget houses; you could start flipping stars.

160. Go Fly a Kite

Windy days were made for taunting electrical storms, seagulls, and other airborne annoyances in pursuit of good old-fashioned grandparent-and-child fun. Build your own U.F.O., or fork out the cash for a lightweight contraption that ignites the imagination and gives wings to your dreams. If you have been remiss in indulging in simple pleasures, the next time someone tells you to *"go fly a kite"* you best heed their advice.

161. Dress Up for a Book / Movie Release

When the latest installment of a blockbuster hits the theatre or bookstore shelves (and your tickle trunk full of your favorite character's signature outfits hasn't been opened in a while) you don't need any encouragement. But if dressing up in anything but your Sunday Best seems sacrilegious, why not let your hair down (or twirl it into *Princess Leia* braids)?

162. Go to a Drive In Movie

Double-features arc double-worth it. They often couldn't be more different than each other (which is what makes it so much fun). You get exposed to another genre / set of actors / themes, so even if the second show turns out to be explicitly graphic or horribly gory, settling in for a night at the drive-in with a blanket and a loved one (or a box of chicken and your favorite intoxicant) at least the first feature is worth every penny.

163. Take Your Grandkids Trick-or-Treating

The best part of Hallowe'en (apart from the whole month leading up to it) is living vicariously through the glow of the kids and their jack-o-lanterns, pillow cases laden with dentist-dissing sugar bombs, who go door-to-door in the only socially-celebrated way these days to be further greeted by gracious hosts who often have as much fun decorating their front doors as the kids have by knocking on them. Just don't let the zombies get you.

164. Swim in Bioluminescence

If you are shy, skinny-dip your toes into the cool water and let the glow swirl around you. It's not magic; it's a natural phenomenon produced by algae blooms, given the perfect conditions. If it's summertime and the weather is easy, put this book down now and go and find those perfect conditions. Why are you still here? Go!

165. Ride a Tandem Bicycle

Call *"shotgun"* so you can ride in the front; otherwise you'll be in for a view of your partner's sweaty navy-striped shirt for your foray along the sea wall; through the forest grove winding through the city park; or up the side of your favorite mountain. And try before you buy, so you don't end up with buyer's remorse if you can't handle those stripes (and your hubby refuses to give up pole position).

166. Find a Four-Leaf Clover

Easier said than done, this author will admit. But don't give up. If you have ever heard *"if there's a will, there's a way"* from your mother (or father) growing up, you of all people may know how possible the impossible just might be. Yes, you may wind up homeless with no friends, money or future, but if you are hell-bent on finding the rarest of leprechaun totems, there is nothing stopping you. Perhaps keep your symbolic quest to yourself.

167. Take Your Grandkids to Your Favorite Spot

Where do you love to be? What physical place feels 'right' to you? Your grandchildren are never too old or young to 'get it', so why not share this special space with them? You may volunteer more (or less) information depending on their age(s), but why not give them a chance to experience a spot that means so much to you?

168. Climb a Tree to the Top

Before you exert yourself beyond what feels reasonably (read: realistically) comfortable to you, go back and read the disclaimer again. On the other hand, if the trunk and branches of that old oak tree are waving you over in a wind storm (and you tend to choose stairs over escalators) don't let a little disclaimer absolving authors and publishers from legal liability stop you from swinging from branch to branch like a monkey.

169. Learn to Say the Alphabet Backwards

If a 3-year-old like Adam Swartz can do it, you can too. Write all the letters out (or use a stencil tool like he did) and practice. Repeating any task will engrain your ability, whether it's something as trivial as learning to say the alphabet backwards, or a much more meaningful faculty like remembering peoples' names the moment you meet them.

170. Carve Your Initials Into a Tree

A pocket knife and a tree with bark are all you need to immortalize your presence at a certain place at a certain time. The tree will grow and age your scrawl (which only give your jagged carvings a more rustic character) so if you feel the need to vandalize nature with graffiti, this is one socially-acceptable way to leave your mark on the world if you never got your 15 minutes of fame for doing some good (or bad).

171. Fill a Charm Bracelet

Often (but not always) geared toward the ladies in the audience, if you already fill / wear a charm bracelet, you are already getting a kick out of your retirement. But for those who aren't, there are no shortage of dangly trinkets available to collect and show off. Just be sure to not to crowd your charms if you are one of the 5 out of 4 people don't understand jokes about math.

172. Win a Talent Show

What can you do that no one else can? Or better: what unique skills / talents do you have that you would be proud to show-off in public? You can finally dust off that old singing saw and demonstrate your prowess without bragging about it (finally a way to get the acknowledgement and approval you've been seeking your whole life). Yodeling, throat singing, ventriloquism and virtuosity in any talent will net you the $25 Grand Prize.

173. Coach Future Athletes

As the team's soccer coach, this author's father used to pull his hair out watching his daughter pick daisies while her peers criss-crossed the field huddled around the ball. But he cheered the loudest when his son scored the only goal of the game one sunny afternoon, winning the league championship for his team. Could you lead little ones to greatness?

174. Watch The Olympics In Person

How many times have you leapt out of your La-Z-Boy celebrating your country's victory in a sporting event reserved for the best-of-the-best? What cultural opening ceremonies and/or exotic destinations have enchanted you? It only happens once every 4 years for a reason, so if it's in your bucket, do it before you kick it.

175. Start a Fire without Matches

There are 3 ways to combine oxygen, spark and flammable material to get fire. #1. Focus a beam of light into a laser through a magnifying glass until your pile of leaves / shredded paper catches fire. #2. Get out the steel wool and pop the hood of your car (not recommended). #3. Rub two pieces of wood together fast enough to create enough heat and spark to ignite a shaved bark tinder nest.

176. Explore a Cave

Who knows what you will find down there. Probably a lot of guano (bat poo), steamy, dripping stalagmites, stalactites, fluvial columns, and a whole lotta I-can't-see-a-thing. Hiring a guide who knows their way around (and who owns - and will share - one of their headlamps) is the way to go, especially if it's your first time crawling around underground. If it turns out you like spelunking, there is no end to the subterranean wonders of the world.

177. Build a Sand Castle

You would be lying if you hadn't attended a Sand Castle competition and been inspired to create a sandy sculpture of your own the next time you were stranded on a long stretch of beach. A modeling medium unlike any other (heated it turns to glass), those fine particles of crushed rock holding various amounts of moisture are waiting to become your fairy tale castle, surrounded with a moat to keep the ne'er do wells where they belong.

178. Go on a Treasure Hunt

Searching for hidden or buried treasure has sparked the imaginations of wayfarers and wanderers ever since loot of any value procured by ill-gotten gains (or honest hard work) had been stashed away and forgotten and/or abandoned. You can scurry your way into treasure-seeking with a $100 metal detector, a GPS, and a curious mind.

179. Beat a Video Game

Did video games ruin your life? Good thing you have 2 left. Before you become a gamer, sit down with your teenage grandkids and share your clueless observations as they hijack cars and race to the finish line; find the invisible health pack and power up; or stumble across the door to the tower where the lovely princess has been pining longingly for them (understandably) getting impatient. Be with them while they are enjoying themselves.

180. Make a Balloon Animal

It's not as easy as it sounds, but you can figure it out. Get a book from the library or type 'make a balloon animal' into your favorite search engine. Soon you'll be the life of every whippersnapper's birthday party. If you don't know any (but it turns out you have a knack for twisting together rubber critters) hire yourself out and enjoy the supplemental income (even though the best kicks will come from laughter).

180. Start a Business

Avoid the cumulative years of brainstorming, daydreaming, scheming, asking questions and researching all the ways, whys and wherefores of starting a business. The 3 simple steps to starting a business are as follows: #1. Decide who you want to serve. #2. Ask them what they want (not what you think they need). #3. Give it to them. It is really that simple, so don't complicate it. Now go do it.

181. Study Marketing

If there are people who want (and will pay for) what you are offering (and running your own business is something that inspires you) you will find (or blaze) your way to your customers, whether employing traditional tried-and-true methods and 'best practices', or launching creative guerrilla marketing warfare. Either way, if you are determined to market your goods and/or services, you will learn the most effective ways to do it. And then do it.

182. Be a Tour Guide

What places do you know like the back of your hand? What states, provinces, regions or countries fascinate you? Do you like people? Do you love eating where the locals eat? And finding the best deals? Why not leverage this enthusiasm into a small business (if you feel so inspired)? There will always be folks in need of hand-holding who want to explore the world and have more meaningful, exciting adventures. They need people like you.

183. Become a Paid Consultant

You have likely forgotten more about your favorite subject / career / hobby than most people know about it, so how could you leverage this knowledge / skill / life experience / passion into some cold hard cash that would enable you to get a kick out of even more of your retirement? Consultancy is big business, so turn your talents into income by helping others get to where they want to go.

184. Become a Life Coach

Leading by example is the best way to teach. But people still struggle and need a kick in the pants to help them change their habits. If said souls routinely seek your counsel about living an inspired / creative / successful life (and you welcome their questions and enjoy listening and facilitating their personal and professional growth) then hang your shingle and start coaching people for free.

185. Write and Publish a Children's Book

When your grandkids climb onto your lap, can you create characters out of thin air and weave them in-and-out-of wild and wooly worldly adventures without too much effort? Nowadays, it's easy to put together any type of book. You can either self-publish your simple story, or go after a traditional publisher and sell them on bringing your saga to life. With a little R&D, both are child's play.

186. Sit on Pads, Pets and Plants

If you love animals, houses and/or gardens and enjoy traveling and/or living like a local, you were born to sit on other people's stuff. Advertise in a local paper, let your network of friends and family know what you're up to, or join one of the many online hubs connecting need-ers with want-ers. Gypsy folk will find looking after houses, pets and plants a sweet way to temporarily ground themselves.

187. Buy Something at an Auction

Do you love to scrounge through yard sales or thrift shop aisles? Or salvage and recycle used yet new-to-you items? If this is already your rare porcelain cup of tea, you don't need a GPS to find your way to the city-wide flea market every Saturday morning. Either cherish your new treasure for antiquity, or turn around and sell it for a profit (in which case your new hobby could grow into a business of epic - or humble - proportions).

188. Shoot a Gun

If you still have testosterone coursing through your veins and haven't shot a gun in all your years, don't you think it's time to summon your inner Chuck Norris or James Bond and go postal (in a controlled environment, of course)? Visit your local hunting club or shooting range if you've always wondered what all the fuss what about. Some call discharging gunpowder a healthy addiction.

189. Shoot a Bow and Arrow

If you feel more like Robin Hood than Rambo (or want to source your own wild meat, and are up for the challenge) then this is your sport. But before you go imagining you are Jennifer Lawrence, note she was trained by an Olympic medalist. Requiring a different skill set than those required to use and maintain firearm, becoming competent (if not masterful) as an archer will bestow rewards in direct proportion to the challenge (like most things).

190. Make a Short Film

A Super 8, VHS, handheld camcorder or the video camera on your phone is all you need to capture light and sound and make your short film. If you want to script, light, decorate, edit, score and release your short film, festivals abound to screen your tale (the trick is getting accepted). But as a retiree, why not play the age card and see what happens?

191. Learn a Musical Instrument

If everything is made of light and sound, does that mean music comes from the stuff of the universe? True or not, music is a powerful form of emotional and creative expression. And because it's never too late to start something new (especially if you have always wanted to) there is room among the star-stuff for you. Start with a ukulele or recorder (just like in elementary school) and practice 10 minutes a day. The more you play, the better you will get. And the better you get, the more you will play.

192. Write a Song

Melody, harmony, rhythm and rhyme combined become what we know and love as songs. You can hum a tune, bang on a pot, or put some rice in a yogurt container. There are no rules. There are no rules. Go back to school. Be cool. Be a fool. You're a molecule. Remember: when it comes to creating something out of nothing, there are no rules.

193. Record a Song

With all the technology available to wannabe recording engineers today, if you have written a song (or 10) and want to record it or them, you can. If you have a Mac, before you open *Garageband* you have been warned: your life will never be the same. If you have a PC, the free program *Audacity* is your tool. Buy an inexpensive USB microphone and go for it. At first, you may not like the sound of your voice on your recording. Secondly, you may never get used to it.

194. Perform a Song

Delusions of grandeur aside, if you want to get up on stage and sing or play a song, do it. Find a venue where skill / talent / experience are optional (an open mic) in a tiny town where no one knows you, and let 'er rip! What's the worst that can happen? Most people are too polite to boo you off the stage, and this ain't *The Gong Show,* so have fun and pretend you're auditioning for *American Idol.*

195. Paint a Picture

If you're serious, go the art store. If you just want to play, go to the dollar store. Both will supply you with what you need to paint your masterpiece. Don't expect offers from art dealer to come pouring in next week (that's not what this is about, unless people end up liking your work). Just start expressing yourself with colors, shapes and textures and see what happens. You may learn something about yourself (wouldn't that be nice).

196. Make Folk Art

It's called folk art because it's made by folks.
Akin to folk? Feel you may have a folky bone in your folky body? Close your eyes and imagine something that doesn't exist. Now make it. There is no end to the materials you can combine / alter / shape / distort / color / enhance / manipulate / destroy in your pursuit of artistic expression (nor tools you can't employ to realize / materialize your creative vision). Wear safety gear and enjoy yourself.

197. Write a Play

What has happened to you that would make a good story? What tragedies and/or comedies have shaped you into who you are? Whether you write (and star in) a one-person show (or see an entire production taking place in your mind's eye) people are hungry for entertaining, enlightening community theatre performances. All begin with a script. Written by someone. Now is your chance. Pen your play today.

198. Learn Photography

Unless you were born yesterday, you have taken a photo (or 10,000) in your life. But are they any good? Yes, the family reunion at Niagara Falls was literally overflowing with magical moments, but haven't you ever wanted to shoot some professional-quality photographs? If so, take a short course and snap away.

199. Create a Cartoon Character

Creating your own cartoon character is a craft, regardless of age or ability. Even if you think you can't draw, start off scribbling or doodling with pen, pencil, crayon or felt. If you have professionally creative friends, borrow a tablet and ask for a quick tutorial. Remember to name your scribble or doodle and assign it a composite personality of all the traits you love and hate about yourself and other people. Forgive this author for opening the flood gates.

200. Learn To Paraglide

Ever wanted to make-like-a-bird and fly? You can launch one of these puppies with your feet and float free, soaring like you have wings in the updraft of the jet stream. Imagine gazing out over your kingdom. Still nervous? Want the rush but a little security in your backpack? Take a short tandem ride and earn your wings before you throw yourself off a cliff without a net.

201. Ride a Snowboard

Remember when the only way you could get down a snowy mountain pronto was on skis? Or maybe a toboggan was more your speed. Nevertheless, once upon a time, a lonely ski mated with a surfboard and gave birth to a snowboard. But don't tell a skier they were responsible (to them, snowboards should have been aborted in the first trimester).

202. Paint Your Self Portrait

If you are reading this, you have considered the possibility. So what are you waiting for? Get out the pens or paints and your mirror on the wall, and let's see if you really are the fairest one of all. Skill or not, why not give it a try? What's the worst that can happen? Sketch until you capture a likeness of your inner angel glowing from within (knowing when to stop is devilishly hard).

203. Get Your Groove On

Whatever you like in your cup (stay away from the mushroom tea) there is a music festival celebrating every genre, style and instrument. Don't worry about standing out as a weird old person; pride yourself in the fact your life experience gives you the wherewithal to not ditch everything and cult-follow your favorite band across the country. Want an experience? Pitch your tent at the Kerrville Music Festival for 18 straight days of folk-tinged tunes.

204. Start a Journal

Dear Diary,

Expressing your thoughts and feelings about your actions and impressions (whether on paper or on your computer) helps to reduce and relieve stress. A journal is a safe place to rant and rave (but only if you get one with a lock on it). Just don't swallow or throw away the key after you have divulged your deepest, darkest secrets.

Sincerely,
Your Name Here

205. Take a Photo a Day for a Year

If you don't do this, one year from now you will have 365 less photos than if you do this. After reviewing your trajectory over the course of one roundabout the sun, you may just marvel at how meaningful and substantial (at least the last year of) your life has been.

206. Carve a Jack-o-Lantern

Gutting and carving a benevolent / malevolent face into the best-selling model of squash is matched perhaps only by making Valentine cards, hiding Easter eggs, or decorating the Christmas tree. Holiday traditions span the ages, symbols of nostalgic wonder and delight, so line your front porch, stairwell or driveway with glowing faces that kids of all ages will enjoy every October 31st.

207. Fold Paper

It all started with paper airplanes and 'fortune tellers' in elementary school, though few graduate to crafting pop-up cards and giving wings to Origami cranes. But then comes paper sculpture, where flattened and dried wood pulp is transformed into intricate 3-dimensional designs worthy of framing. But the secret to creating art is knowing when to stop, because (apparently) folding a piece of paper 103 times will dwarf the universe.

208. Create a Vision Board

A vision board (also known as a 'treasure map' in new-age circles) is a glorified collage filled with photos and phrases from magazines that represent the desires / goals / dreams you want to achieve / attain / make happen. This piece of art is supposed to remind your non-conscious mind of what you want, so you will notice when the breadcrumbs (clues) appear. Hippies.

209. Make a Pop–Up Birthday Card

If you are artistically inclined, pop-up cards are a piece of cake. Tutorials abound in the numerous books housed in numerous libraries. What are books? You are reading one. What is a library? A place with free books. Be patient with yourself and buy the paper in bulk (you will have some casualties as you wrap your head around the physics of inverse ratios and other geometric realities / impossibilities.

210. Capture Lightning on Camera

Lightning is simply a discharge that equalizes electrically-charged regions, either within the clouds, or between the clouds and the ground. And photography is about 2 things: lighting and composition (if you have a flash on your camera you are playing god). But tread lightly, storm-chaser, and wear rubber boots when you go puddle jumping in an electrical storm. This ain't no live fence back on the farm.

211. Be a Movie Extra

Bring a book, because your bum will get sore waiting for the production assistant (read: shepherd) to herd you and the other sheep onto the set. Unless they fly you to some exotic location (or it's an action movie) you may as well bring a blanket and a pillow. On top of that, don't expect to rub elbows with Brad Pitt or Amy Adams; they have people whose job it is to keep people like you from rubbing elbows with them. Sounds glamorous, doesn't it?

212. Build a Train Set

What do you know about building a train set? Nothing? Then get chugging. Old toy trains have gone the way of the tape deck, so why not construct a mag-lev train instead? Riding on nothing but air, these bullet trains zoom inches above their rails, leavened by little more than magnetic tension. Being the last person on earth interested in antique toys, you might try your luck at an estate sale.

213. Race Radio–Controlled Cars

Deep down, did you never really grow up? George Bernard Shaw said *"we don't stop playing because we get old; we get old because we stop playing."* A hobby store (read: toy store for adults) will let you browse to your heart's content before deciding to buy / build / modify / race / trash-talk your own radio-controlled car (or truck) around the track and into the winner's circle (read: glorified sandbox).

214. Buy and Sell Antiques

Whether dealing in antiques seems like global big business or a leisurely weekend pursuit, if you aren't already poring over buyer's guides and blowing dust off of under-appreciated treasures at Saturday morning yard sales, what are you waiting for? And in the rare case your social life could use a little restoration, it turns out that people who like antiques like people who like antiques.

215. Learn a New Language

How did you learn your first language? Forget classrooms, textbooks and quizzes; get yourself an audio program and give it 30 minutes a day. 30 days later you will be ordering food; asking the server for his or her phone number; telling him or her off when he or she rejects you; and directing a cab driver back to your hotel where you can watch late-night soap operas sans subtitles and be okay with it all.

216. Hunt for UFOs

Get yourself a video camera, a notebook and (to avoid any confusion) a flight plan from your local airport. Now find a bit of sky to stake-out and wait... There could be billions of habitable planets in galaxies not too far away (!) so don your tin-foil hat and join your favorite ufology organization before you get beamed up and forget to leave a note for your next of kin letting them know you are planning to be gone a while. The worst (or best) case scenario is that (apparently) you don't age in outer space.

217. Steal a Kiss

As long as you aren't creepy about it, turning on the charm and smooching with a complete angel (or ogre) will either get you smacked or shacked-up. So pucker up buttercup, because you could strike anywhere at anytime. No one is safe from your wayward lips!

218. Read the Books on Your Bookshelf

How long have they been collecting dust? And how long have you been meaning to read them? First of all, you are not alone, so take heart: the books want to be read as much as you want to read them. And now you are retired, you have all the time in the world to do the things you have never had time to do. Need a little help? If you were stranded on a desert island, what is the one book you could enjoy reading over and over again?

219. Be a Snowbird

The world is a big place, if you didn't know it already, and weather to suit all sorts abounds. So if you don't like when your face freezes (or worse: you have never got a kick out of putting yourself at increased risk for a heart-attack while shoveling your driveway for the nth time this week) do like the birds do: put your affairs in order and fly south for the winter.

220. Get Your Pilot's License

As long as you are physically able, take to the skies and learn to fly. Just log the hours, complete the training and pass the tests. Wait. Is getting your pilot's license and buying / insuring / licensing / fueling your own plane too much of a budgetary stretch? Start piloting ultralights, or go where the breeze takes you on a colorful hang-glider with no floor, walls, radio, autopilot or black box.

221. Go Zorbing

Now the subject of a major motion picture, Bubble Boy was the pioneer of what is now known as globe-riding / sphereing / orbing / zorbing (rolling down a hill inside an orb of transparent plastic). Bubble Boy was deprived on an immune system (and thus lived his life within his own ecosphere) so if you generally feel misunderstood, at least the projectiles and insults would bounce right off.

222. Break a World Record

If you haven't already broken a World Record, your chances are getting slimmer every day (unless you have been slowly growing your fingernails for the past few years hoping to beat the standing record of 8.65 meters). Not there yet? Hang-nail on for 122 years and 165 days (1 day longer than the current record holder for 'oldest person'). Belief is the best guarantee.

223. Go To War

Stuffing ferns into your helmet to camouflage your existence on the forest floor (or perching yourself high in a tree top waiting to snipe your unsuspecting enemies with paint) may be the closest you ever come to experiencing life on the battlefield. Guaranteed to get your blood pumping, firing semi-automatic weapons at your friends and sending them home bruised and beaten (after you capture the flag and rescue the princess) is heart-pounding.

224. Hit a Home Run

If you have been playing baseball or softball for any length of time and have yet to hit a home run, put this book down, and don't come back until you knock one out of the park. On the other hand, if you have never stepped foot on a baseball diamond (but have always wanted to) join a Seniors Slow Pitch league and step up to the plate. Batter up!

225. Go Horseback Riding

People have been riding horses almost as long as people and horses have coexisted, so you are in good company if you want to giddy up and go trail or ring riding (or even take to the high plains on a multi-day trek, guided of course). So pack your saddle bags, sharpen your spurs, fill your canteen with your favorite outdoor brew and ride into the sunset, because you're not getting any younger, cowboy.

226. Develop Your Psychic Powers

Whether you want to persuade someone to do your bidding, or simply dial into another dimension and communicate with non-physical beings, you have the capacity to connect to infinite intelligence / collective unconscious / invisible source (whatever you want to call it). Interested? You won't find this place on *Google Maps*, so let your 6th sense guide you once you tame your monkey mind with deep breathing exercises.

227. Learn Sign Language

Learning American Sign Language goes beyond memorizing signs. Infused with its own culture, history and grammar rules, you can quickly become a skilled language user by investing a little time and effort every day adopting your new skill set. Beginning with signs for: family / places / time / food / feelings / requests / colors / money / animals will be easier than reading lips.

228. Play The Didgeridoo

Believed to be the world's oldest wind instrument, the vibrating drone sound of 'the didge' began enchanting aborigines in Northern Australia thousands of years ago. What follows is the condensed 'how to' version adapted from 3 different instructors: relax your face, puff up your cheeks up with air, let your loose lips sink into the tube, create an air-tight seal and blow. Now you do it.

229. Audition for a Play

Shakespeare said *"all the world's a stage, and all the men and women merely players."* In other words, you are already acting and playing your part; so why not go public? Theatre people are generally happy, creative, productive folks who know how to laugh and have fun. FYI: Your local theatre company is always looking for new talent (even you just want to stand there like a tree).

230. Sing in a Choir

Rock and roll, religious or soul. Whatever you like to sing, a choir is waiting for your angelic tenor, soothing counter-tenor, ear-piercing soprano, humble second-in-command mezzo-soprano, supportive alto, booming baritone, or how-low-can-you-go bass. Wait. You don't know how to sing? Nor do most people. That's what lip-syncing is for.

231. Learn to Sew

Home Economics in middle school wasn't too long ago, was it? You remember how to thread the bobbin, right? Now, the hardest part will be choosing the correct color of thread. But clothes, curtains and car-covers alike, draping your life with fabric is a creative endeavor. As such, you are encouraged to let your fashion sense fly in the face of convention and to experiment with shapes, sizes, colors, patterns and textures.

232. Learn to Knit

Chances are your grandmother taught you how to knit (if not your great aunt). Like any hobby, you can bet others with similar interests share your personality traits. And in case you haven't noticed, enjoying your retirement involves either making friends, expressing yourself in creative ways, exploring your inner and outer worlds, and/or having fun. So darn it if you drop a stitch.

233. Crack The Code

Apart from working for an intelligence agency as a cryptologist, why not decrypt the code to ultimate joy and happiness? If you are hell-bent on getting a kick out of retirement by earning a little extra money, ask yourself: what do you love so much you would do it for free? The answer to this question is also the key to life; decipher the code and you will have the answer to everything that matters.

234. Burn Some Paper Money

Viva la revolución! More an affirmation of personal prosperity than an act of treason, torching just 5 bucks will profoundly (temporarily) change the way you view money, and the inherent value you give to your personal resources. It's nice to see things differently once in a while (especially if you worry about not having enough). *"The best things in life are free"* is a cliché because it's true.

235. Do Calligraphy

We are surrounded with alphabets in varying fonts, styles and designs (and languages, depending on where we live). Grab a pen and paper and write your name. Now pretend the wispy wind is carrying it away (draw swirls from the tops of the first and last letters), or imagine your name taking root and flourishing with tiny leaves and elegant embellishments. Take a class or mimic what you see online.

236. Paint a Mural

Professionals sketch an outline before attempting their masterpiece (you are advised to do the same). Start with a wall in your house so when the big leagues beckon, your portfolio will impress your wall-owner client before you go mucking up their drive-in theatre-sized canvas. Though if somehow the city is already commissioning you to splash your art across public spaces, keep going.

237. Bedazzle Yourself

Jewelry doesn't have to be expensive. With a little ingenuity and creativity you can make (and show off) your bling on a limited budget. Too lazy? Head down to your local thrift store and peruse their endless display cases of previously loved tokens of artificial wealth. Remember to lower your nose when you walk in the front door and acknowledge the greeter (you're likely in a strip-mall secondhand store, not *Tiffany & Co.*)

238. Learn Your Love Language

The 5 'love languages' refer to the ways you communicate and express your love for the people around you. Seemingly accurate and quite evocative, you will soon know whether your primary communication style entails physical touch, words of encouragement, quality time, acts of service, or gifts.

239. Play Heavy Metal

Banging on and shaping red hot steel with handheld sledge hammers to forge tools and other practical conveniences is a pastime as old as the raw elements themselves. Recent revival of this heavy-duty hobby has taken the shape of functional household utensils like cutlery and serving bowls, in addition to coat hangers, tables and furniture. Your local blacksmith association (like most hobby-associated associations) will welcome you with open tongs, so don't be shy.

240. Get Drunk on Water

While water is considered to be one of the least toxic chemical compounds, drinking too much of life's most essential liquid can disrupt the balance of electrolytes in your body and result in water poisoning (ouch!) and be potentially fatal (eek!) so don't try this at home. And while death from hyper-hydration is rare, you can guard against any and all adverse effects by drinking this abundant substance in moderation.

241. Fix Your Grandfather's Watch

If you can keep your hands steady (and enjoy working with tiny tools, gears, motors, rotors, switches and dials; have a lit magnifying glass on a swivel arm; plus a nice place to work on your grandfather's timeless timepiece) put on your lab coat and pretend you're Dr. Frankenstein on a mission to bring your antique back to life. The clock is ticking.

242. Build a Computer

If you want to build a computer, this book is not the place to learn. So where do you start? Go to a friendly computer store and ask *them*. Just like the many other witty ways in this book concocted to help you get a kick out of retirement, this short paragraph is simply another attempt to inspire you / motivate you / tempt you / tease you / repeatedly kick-you-in-the-pants until you get off your bum and try something (anything) new.

243. Build a Website

With all the free (ad-supported) ways to build your own website on the inter-webs, there is no excuse to go unnoticed if you have something to say or to sell to the world. 571 websites appear online *every minute*. What is a little competition? Just think: this is only the beginning. Tip: spend a few dollars a month and get your own domain name if you want to be taken seriously.

244. Put in a Swimming Pool

First of all, you need a yard (and your spouse's permission) before you go hiring someone to dig the hole and you start dreaming of tanned beauties parading around the pool in their bikinis (or the more-wholesome imaginings of family fun taking place in your backyard every weekend from now on). Either way, know that your in-laws will eventually desecrate your holy water park in one way or another.

245. Feed The Hummingbirds

Colorful quick little creatures that flutter their wings around 50 times per second, hummingbirds are beautiful birds to watch. You can lure them over to your place with sugar water (homemade or store-bought) in molded plastic bird feeders that look like flowers. Like most living things, hummingbirds are attracted to the color red, so tie a ribbon around their favorite fast food outlet and you will get noticed more often.

246. Do Your Own Laundry

If you've had a maid / spouse / partner do your laundry your whole life, roll up your sleeves and check the pockets of your pants. Follow the instructions on the washing liquid label, because you need less than you think. Separating whites, colors and delicates is how *not* to get a kick out of retirement, so skip it and learn to rock pink socks.

247. Build a Tree House

Most importantly you must pick the right tree(s): oak, beech, maple, ash, hemlock, cedar or Douglas fir. Some consider the stress hardware such as anchor bolts will put on their trees, but as long as you have a plan (no need for a structural engineering degree) you can build a safe, beautiful, cozy tree house that will last a lot longer than you (and be enjoyed for years to come by the ones you love). For those you aren't so fond of, building the trap door will be the best part.

248. Build a Tiny House

Not only easier and more affordable to build than a conventional house, a tiny house is also easier to keep clean and move around. Books and blogs abound on tiny houses and the people who build them and love them. Finally, if you are in need (or want) of affordable housing and have access to the required skills (and the whole idea of appeals to you) you may soon know the freedom, joy and simplicity of 'living small'.

249. Build Willow Furniture

With a few tools and a little creativity, you can build a simple table or chair in a day. Start gathering branches in the Spring, and keep in mind you need thick ones for the legs, and varying lengths for the arms / back / table top. You can get detailed instructions online, or in your local bookstore / library. Building willow furniture is practical (and a practical use of your precious time).

250. Build a Canoe

Hollow out an old tree trunk by hand; glue together some slats of wood; or make a mold and fiberglass resin-together your humble sailing ship. Remember: the hardest ships to destroy are friendships, so when you're done, chart out a route and recruit a second mate to test this theory (and your canoe) and go paddling down the river with you.

251. Renovate Your Kitchen

If you spend more time in your kitchen than anywhere else, and have been wanting to renovate / upgrade it for some time, only attempt a DIY project if you know what you're doing (otherwise you'll be eating take-out for longer than you like). Better yet, hire a professional contractor / big box store to help. You still get to compromise with your spouse following heated debates over the design, appliances, materials and colors (you know, the fun part).

252. Plant a Garden

This author has oft been wrangled into digging up front yards when his friends proclaimed they wanted 'food not lawns'. Hopefully you aren't as ecologically militant as said 'friends' so leave your lawn alone, and dig up a 6x6 plot in a sunny corner of your backyard instead. Start with good soil, grow some local organic food, and give yourself the gift of health.

253. Plant a Tree

Trees clean the air and supply us with oxygen. They also provide shade in the summer and wondrous beauty in the winter, covered with snow or twinkly lights. You could plant a tree in memory of someone or something, or just because you want an organic fence between you and your nosy neighbors. If you like free food: plant an apple, pear, plum, peach, cherry, almond, avocado, pomegranate, walnut, apricot, lemon or lime tree.

254. Grow Facial Hair

Easy for men, yet not so socially-acceptable for women (although some ladies rock the stash or uni-brow). The tormented artist Frida Kahlo did, for sure (which is maybe why she was so tormented). For guys going bald, facial hair is the last frontier (and remaining semblance of masculine pride) so braid or dread-lock a beard, grow a tough handle-bar mustache, sport a neat goatee, or trim yourself a groovy soul patch.

255. Grow Your Hair Long

Why on earth if not to grow? Man or woman, long hair gives you options. Yes, it's more work to wash, dry, style, cut and maintain, but maybe it's worth it. Some cultures believe that long hair is an extension of your thoughts, and that those with long hair are less likely to become depressed. And if you were created in the image of JC, why not show it?

256. Play a Song on the Piano

Learning to play any instrument takes time. But the more you play, the better you get, and the better you get, the more you will want to play (it's a vicious cycle). In case you didn't know, most of your favorite songs are only 3 chords, so unless your suffer from a severe learning disability, you can learn to play your favorite song in a day. Caveat: if you don't know the tune and lyrics by heart (and can't sing along) it may take a week. Oh, and you need a piano.

257. Study Latin

Thanks to a hungry-for-culture whim while in high school, this author asked an elderly scholar to teach him Latin. Near useless these days, if your lips yearn to speak this ancient language, do what your lips want. Yes, latin verbs may only come in handy in the forgone catacombs of civilization, but if nothing else in this book turns you on, carpe diem!

258. Restore an Old Car

If restoring an old car to its former glory turns your camshaft and gets your motor running, you know what to do. Again: if something ignites the fuel in your cylinders (the auto references are too easy) give your hotrod a new paint job, put the top down and burn some rubber. Don't expect it to be easy or affordable, but you can find replacement parts for any vehicle. If there is a will, there is a way.

259. Buy a Convertible

You are well past the date of a mid-life crisis, so there is no stigma attached to buying a convertible and enjoying the sun on your face, the wind through your hair, and the bugs, dust, rain and rubbish that will spoil your scenic coastal cruise. As this author's late grandfather used to say *"there are pros and cons to everything. You can't have one without the other."* But don't let his wizened wisdom spoil your fun: convertibles are a blast.

260. Buy a Motorcycle

Have you seen those panniers (saddle bags) and mini trailers that bikers tow? Some people ride their laden motorbikes across countries regardless of ill terrain, weather, climate, amenities and lack (or abundance) of locals. Truly a romantic adventure, it all begins with at the bike shop. But you want the sizzle, not the steak (which is why this way to get a kick out of retirement began like it did).

261. Go to Expensive Open Houses

If you believe in the power of a focused mind to plant inner seeds (the results of which you can later materialize and thus reap) going to expensive open houses is an essential piece of what this author calls *Creative Sensation*. If you are at all inclined towards the Law of Attraction, you know the more you stimulate your senses while 'experiencing' the end result in your imagination, the faster you will realize your dreams.

262. Ride in a Limo

All you need are some friends or family to split the cost of a few hours in a limo (note: you will have more fun with the former). Drive around town, go to a favorite look-out, go winery-hopping, or be tourists in your own town. The experience will be as exotic as you make it, so don some sleek and stylish duds, drink some champagne, crank the tunes, pop-out of the sunroof, and wave your hands in the air like you just don't care. Then post the pictures and videos online and make everyone jealous.

263. Ride a Vespa

A *vespa* is an Italian scooter (if their scooters are anything like their sports cars, you are in for a treat, for vespa means wasp in Italian). But you don't need to go to Italy to buzz around town looking for people to piss off (there are probably people in your own neighborhood you can happily annoy). Just wear a helmet and take it easy, Mario Andretti.

264. Drive a Ferrari Across Italy

You will have a more authentic experience if you are actually in Italy for this one. But you don't need to take out a bank loan to rent your favorite model of the sexiest cars on the planet; just cash-in your life insurance policy and be done with it. Because what is more important: providing for your loved ones after ironically being turned away at the gates of heaven, or living life like a sexy Italian supermodel / rockstar / dictatorial despot for a week in the boot of the Mediterranean?

265. Eat Caviar

It remains a mystery to this author why salt-cured fish eggs are such a delicacy (maybe it's because he didn't grow up with a silver spoon full of fish roe to munch on as an appetizer). Then again, as this author's obviously liberally-quoted grandfather used to say: *"all the more for those who like it."*

266. Fly in a Private Jet

At only a few thousand dollars an hour, a private jet is the way to fly. If you can't stand economy (and business class feels too elitist) scrap public transportation all together and do like the string-pullers of the world do and get to where you're going hassle-free, on-time, and with all the perks and comforts of home. The best part? You never have to pay extra to check your baggage which will probably go AWOL anyway.

267. Stop Worrying

Worry is a wish for what you don't want (and therefore the greatest threat to getting a kick out of your retirement. So whenever worry wriggles its way into your weekend, armed with malicious intent to wreck your life, bolt the door and remember this: as long as you are dwelling on what will likely not happen, there is no room in your life for magic, miracles, happiness, friendship and love.

268. Win Something

Get yourself on a game show; enter every marketing lead-generation survey / draw / lottery / sweepstakes / contest you can. Increase your odds of winning and you will (eventually) win. Free stuff, competitions and raffles are everywhere, eager for your participation / email address / thoughts. But stay away from casinos, because it's true: the house always wins.

269. Take The Waters in Karlovy Vary

Thermal mineral springs called colonnades well-up out of the ground in this cute little touristy spa town in the Czech Republic, not far from the German border. Overflowing with tourists, yes, but for good reason: its waters are reputed for their healing and therapeutic benefits. 'Vary'-ing in temperature, the springs regularly ease all gastrointestinal disorders (or maybe it's just the placebo effect).

270. Lease a Luxury Vehicle

Now you can live the dream for only $X per month on a X-month term at X% financing (all you need is the desire and cash / credit to qualify). Shell out enough shekels and you can hire a chauffeur, because leasing luxury is what money is for. But when everything in life is temporary, the question becomes: are we simply 'renting' our bodies / homes / families / friends / thoughts / feelings / possessions / experiences / memories?

271. Sleep in Silk Sheets

The higher the thread-count the better, they say, but silk sheets still get a bad wrap. Contrary to popular belief, they don't require dry-cleaning; won't shrink in the laundry; are not chemically-processed; and will last a while (provided you don't get too rough in the sack with your favorite person). So slip into some silk sheets and live like a royal for a while.

272. Cover Up The Price

Visit the highest-rated joint you can find and cover up the price trash-talking you from the sidebar. Better yet, ask the server-in-the-know for their recommendation and pair your many divine courses with complementing (not complimentary - not yet) wine choices and savor. Every. Single. Bite. The same goes for the grocery store. Try this 'abundance' strategy for a week. Buy what you (and your body) want to eat, and watch what it does to your self-esteem.

273. Buy a Nice Watch

Advertised everywhere, countless brands of watches beg you to buy and wear them. Yes, you know you are being brainwashed, for they attract you in one way or another. And when all you have is time, why not keep track of your most precious resource in style? Just look after it, so great-great-grand-junior will appreciate it even more when it's inevitably his.

274. Get a Mani-Pedi

For the gentlemen in the audience unversed in the traditional domain of women, a mani-pedi is short for a manicure and pedicure (having your fingernails and toenails polished and treated in one visit). Guys: your fingernails and toenails need love too, so pick up the phone, book an appointment and go. If you're scared, ask a loving lady in your life to hold your hand.

275. Bake a Layer Cake

Not a baker? Buy a mix, your favorite flavor / color of icing, and some cheap cake pans. Follow the instructions on the box and do your best to slice them into layers once they cool. Alternate frosting and cake (be gentle; they are fragile) until you are satisfied with the result. Even as an amateur baker, a creatively decorated cake will always surprise and delight everyone gathered to celebrate a special occasion (even if it's 'just because'). The fun is worth the fattening part.

276. Get Drunk Before Lunch

Mimosas anyone? It seems champagne and orange juice were made for each other, so don't feel bad if every Sunday you find an excuse to celebrate something as simple as a perfect Sunday morning (substituting cranberry, grape, mango or pomegranate juice is perfectly acceptable). The more the merrier, so send out the invitations.

277. Get Rich Quick

You can get rich quick (you just have to get lucky and find something that pays off in a short time (like the stock market) and stay out of trouble, so you can enjoy the fruits of your labour. Adventurous folks have been timing (read: playing) the stock market since there was a stock market. All you need is a head for numbers; the uncanny ability to see the future; the courage to stake your disposable income on your hypotheses; and a reckless Vegas-or-bust attitude and tolerance for risk.

278. Own 100 Pairs of Shoes

How many pairs of shoes does *anyone* really need? If the answer is: *"you can never have too many"* (and you don't already own 100 pairs) be honest with yourself: the lack of precious closet space is not the issue. If overall dissatisfaction with life in general is the real problem, the solution is temporary: shopping your way to shoe heaven will only relieve the symptoms for a while. On the other hand, when (lack of) space appears to be the problem, simply 'tidy' up your spouse's side of the closet to make room for your 100th pair of kicks.

279. Buy Something on TV

If your favorite shopping channel is advertising an item (or bundle) 'on sale for a limited time only' and you MUST have it NOW, pull out the plastic, because they may sell out fast, and then what will you do? (Hint: either wait a week, or go channel surfing).

280. Take an All-Inclusive Vacation

All-Inclusive means feet are the only requirement (unless you go in the pool, in which case you are advised to use your arms to stay afloat / alive). Everything else is taken care of (except the timeshare salespeople who will offer to take care of a portion of your bank account for the next 20 years). Regardless of what you have heard, these friendly folks play ingenious separate-tourist-from-their-money mind games that too-often result in you being separated from your money (the free buffet lunch or scenic tour of the ruins is not worth it).

281. Get Married in Las Vegas

If you're in the marriage capital of the world to party, drink up. If you're there to gamble, good luck. And if you're there to get married, wake up. The Chinese proverb says: *"If you want to be happy for a week, get married. If you want to be happy for a lifetime, plant a garden."*

281. Get Backstage at a Show

Meeting your favorite singer / musician / actor / comedian / comedienne is a blast. They are popular and famous for a reason: they are often charismatic, intelligent, outgoing and friendly. So when you do wrangle a backstage pass and get to meet your hero / heroine, maintain your composure and you will be fine. Just remember to use your words instead of your tears... of joy.

282. Get Someone's Autograph

The someone doesn't have to be famous, necessarily (although the more famous they are, the more props you will get from your friends and family when you show off your vandalized T-shirt, glossy 8x10, or desecrated body part). What is behind the power of an autograph? Some people believe that signatures leave behind an energetic 'residue' which is 'imbued' with the signee's aura. Believe what you want.

283. Enjoy Breakfast in Bed

It always tastes better if someone else made if for you (and better still if you get to choose from a menu). Neither option available to you this fine morning? You are either fortunate or unfortunate, depending on how you frame it. Some celebrate the single life, whereas others damn it daily. Either way: dishwashers, egg poachers, packets of powdered Hollandaise sauce, frozen croissant dough, and not-from-concentrate orange juice are passable consolation prizes.

284. Ride in a Submarine

Don't ask this author how you get to do this (it just seemed like another neat way to get a kick out of retirement) unless you aren't stuck on riding in an *actual* sub-sea vessel. Like most suggestions in this book, you can always pretend things are different than they are (even when they aren't). Use your imagination because retirement is playtime.

285. Judge a Beauty Contest

Some think not even the big guy upstairs is capable of judging what we get up to down here on the mud ball we call earth. Though if you have been called from on high (the 3-foot stage) to sit among a panel of experts and doth one young lady the reigning beauty of your county fair or beauty pageant, take the responsibility seriously, for this is an honor when beauty is in the eye of the beer-holder.

286. Become an Arms Dealer

There are 3 things you need to be an arms dealer: balls (or the female equivalent), guns (or the ability to get them), and a complete disregard for both the suffering of humankind and the ecological degradation of the planet. Enough of the above (to at least fund the start-up years) will ensure your life rife with rifles will be safe and sound, the armory under your pillow lulling you to sleep instead of a stuffy (unless it's a G.I. Joe doll armed to the hilt).

287. Buy Season's Tickets to the Symphony

Want to get out of the trailer park more often? Mingling with high society ain't the best part of holding season's tickets to the symphony; the music is transcendental. Why let commercial radio relentlessly bludgeon you into sonic submission for which you have zero to little tolerance? 'Symphony' is another word for 'culture'.

288. Live in Tuscany for a Year

Oh, olive trees, fresh tomatoes, lavender fields and wineries. The rustic bread and the fresh pasta. Care not if you don't parlare (speak) Italian; the only 3 words you need to know are *"Delicious; yes; thank you"*. Little else matters in the land of sun and slow. If the warm wind doesn't sing you to sleep while starry skies keep and your favorite person dazzled in dreamland for hours, there is no hope for you. Pack up and go home.

289. Attend The Festival de Cannes

Admission to the annual film (fashion) festival in France is by invitation only, so unless your people know people who know people, don't bet on getting in. If you dare aspire to rubbing elbows with cinema's elite, then simply script / produce / direct / score / edit and/or star in a film that gets screened at this most prestigious festival. All other methods risk public disgrace.

290. Get Box Seats

Arts and sporting events alike allow for matrons, patrons and fans of all ages and abilities to segregate themselves from the common peasants in reserved box seats while they watch their favorite entertainers win, lose, rejoice and suffer at the hands of their counterparts via various acts of violence, drama, action and romance. It's up to you how you want to spend your time entertaining (read: showing-off to) your homies.

291. Bake a Soufflé

Don't sweat the soufflé. If you can whip cream, you can please the crowd with only a handful of ingredients. The basics: carefully separate your eggs; whip the whites at a 45 degree angle until stiff; gently fold them into the yolk custard or sauce. Simply use high-quality ingredients, read the recipe, take your time, and have fun. Sweet or savory, you got this.

292. Find a Pearl

If you want to find a pearl, go where the pearls are. Hire a guide to take you diving, or try your luck down at your local buck-a-shuck (though this is a long-shot). If you do find one, they tend to be misshapen and look more like little pebbles than rocks (that's what you get for taking a shortcut). Beware: don't lose a tooth on your bi-valve hunting trip, because your dentist is likely to refuse payment in shiny pebbles.

293. Use Valet Parking

Why would anyone would pay to park when they could walk a mile instead? Because it's convenient (and goes a long way to impress a gold-digging date with dubious values). Pay parking is a luxury, and now that you are retired, you deserve a splurge. Still, your money is better off in your savings account than funding the valet's bag of marijuana or tuition installment. Remember: if you don't want to park your own car, glance at the odometer when you drop it off and do the math when you get it back.

294. Laugh on Command

Being prompted to laugh as a member of a live TV show audience when the APPLAUSE sign starts flashing is like being trained to salivate like Pavlov's dog when you hear the bell ring. Then again, 99% of us were trained to stand at attention / corral ourselves / come inside when the bell rang in the first grade.

295. House Swap

House swapping is the next best thing to living a double life (but without the inevitable stress, anxiety, lies and dishonesty). You get to live someone else's life for a while, and even walk in their shoes. But read the fine print: their liquor cabinet may be fair game, though their 100-shoe collection stashed in their closet may be off-limits. Keep in mind that if you go rummaging through their stuff, chances are they are having just as much fun at your place.

296. Go to a Full Moon Party

Unless you thrive on risk and seek an authentic experience, refuse open beverages from friendly-faced strangers. As in any unfamiliar situation, don't haunt yourself with nightmares; full moon parties are excuses to let yourself go in the safe clutches of ecstatic dance, trusting that all is well with the world. Without the freedom to dance like no one is looking, there is no enjoyment in retirement.

297. Find Your Tribe at Burning Man

Honor the 10 Principles: radical inclusion, gifting, de-commodification, radical self-reliance, radical self-expression, communal effort, civic responsibility, leaving no trace, participation, immediacy; and you are welcome to join in the festivities. Not a cult nor a religion, *Burning Man* is a way of life. If you seek the personification and expression of these values, go find your tribe.

298. Swim with Dolphins

Found in every ocean, dolphins are highly intelligent marine mammals. Friendly and playful, the dolphins in captivity are rented out for tricks and kisses, trained to charm you with their antics and acrobatics. What's that? You want an authentic swimming-with-dolphins experience? Then go find them in the wild. As chaperones to your sea-worthy vessel, you will be giddy with excitement when they appear, urging you to join them playing in the waves.

299. Ride a Camel

First of all, camels are not horses. And don't expect it to be a smooth ride; the bumps hint at what kind of journey you can expect. Riding a camel is easy; it's the lift off and landing that's difficult. Always wondered what it's like to see life from the back of a camel? You don't have to go to Egypt, Morocco, China or Australia. If you live near the Pacific Northwest, call up *Camel Safari* in Bellingham.

300. Roll Across Russia

It took 25 years to build and connect the Trans-Siberian railway (but you can get from one end of the biggest country in the world in about 7 days, unless you stop-off to see some of the breathtaking countryside). For those who would rather not fly from Europe to Asia (or the other way around) why not live on vodka and instant noodles for a week, while reading *War and Peace* and watching the world roll slowly by?

301. Drive from Sea to Shining Sea

Yes, you can get from sea to shining sea in about 5 hours (for the cost of a few tanks of gas) but where is the fun in that? Don't have a travel companion? Post your itinerary on a ride sharing website and make some new friends. You can't rest until you have dipped your toes in the other ocean and seen the sights that make this land great.

302. Raft The Grand Canyon

Admittedly, rafting anywhere is not for everyone (which is why there are safer ways to get kicks out of retirement). Dangerous as river rafting may seem, if you like getting tossed around in small boats in rough water while dodging massive boulders and wayward timbers; experiencing weightless as you go headfirst over waterfalls, this is your sport. Your blood will flow quicker than the rapids. But you won't notice, because the only thing you will hear / think / do / say is *"Paddle!"*

303. Catch Crabs

A fishing license is a license for free food. Why pay $20 for a crab at the grocery store (or more at the fishmongers) when $20 gets you free crab for a year? Yes, you have to handle frozen chicken necks and backs (where crustaceans acquired a taste for the bird no one knows), get yourself a crab trap and zip-ties, and spend some time down at the dock chatting with other seafood lovers. The pros clearly outweigh the cons.

304. Kiss The Blarney Stone

Rumored to endow smoochers with the gift of the gab, millions of visitors (according to castle officials) have kissed the limestone at Blarney Castle. Be warned: you have to climb to the castle peak and lean over backwards (if you fear heights, you may just have to accept your god-given button lips the next time you want to chat someone up).

305. Visit The Holy Land

Pilgrims flock like sheep to the biblical land between the ancient Jordan River and the Mediterranean Sea. Although the birthplace of religion (and thus both historically and culturally mind-blowing) Israel and Palestine are maybe better left well alone. If they can't agree to disagree, why encourage them? On the other hand, the Holy Land may be so (hypocritically) contaminated by literal mind-blowing nuclear fallout one day that no one will want to go. So if it's on your TO DO list, DO it while you can.

306. Get a Divorce

If you are like most people, you can't help but want to be married to someone you love. But if / when the day comes you can't stand to spend another second with love in all its forms (and you have tried everything to make it work) it's okay to give up. But be gentle (with them too) because divorce is beyond stressful.

307. Visit The Statue of Liberty

The copper 'Statue of Liberty Enlightening the World' was a friendly gift from the French in 1886, and has been recognized around the world as a symbol of freedom and democracy ever since (sometimes this author wonders if we should give it back). But as an optimist, you feel lucky to live in a free and democratic society (and trust we haven't lost our way). In this case, you itch to visit her crown the next time you are scratching around the Big Apple, so reserve your advanced tickets online.

308. See Paris from The Eiffel Tower

Ah, Paris. There is no place on earth quite like it (nor few monuments quite like the one Hitler ordered torn down). Thankfully, the French refused (typical) so you can see 42 miles in every direction, given perfect conditions. Pair your view with wine, cheese, a fresh baguette, and the language of love... What else do you need? The French know the answer: *"rien"*.

309. Climb The Great Pyramids

Of the 3 Great Pyramids in Giza, Khufu is easier to climb than the others, though was never a walk-in-the-park at an angle of 51.5 degrees (maybe that's why it's been illegal since the 70's). But if running afoul of sweaty, militarized Middle Eastern authorities doesn't faze you, make like a mountain goat and soldier on. And be sure to stroke your ego afterwards, because for the rest of us, this would be far too much heated excitement for one trip / lifetime.

310. Visit Antarctica

Uninhabited. Covered in ice. Home to more penguins than people. The coldest, driest, windiest, 5th-largest continent on earth can be explored thanks to the 80 companies belonging to *The International Association of Antarctica Tour Operators* (FYI: In the 2005-06 summer season, more than 26,000 people crossed Antarctica off their bucket list).

311. Kick It with The Clauses

As long as you don't book your holiday in December, you can probably get in to see the Big Man himself (otherwise, you will be stuffing your face with gingerbread cookies and getting drunk on candy cane wine and gossiping with Mrs. Claus and her friends). Regardless of the lies your parents touted to keep you in line as a child, there is no such thing as the Naughty List. The Clauses (who actually live in Finland) are lovely, non-judgmental people who delight in introducing visitors to Rudolph and the gang before taking them through the enchanted forest to the workshop where all the magic happens.

312. Step Foot on all 7 Continents

Are you smarter than a 5th-Grader? Can you name the 7 continents? Go! With often nothing more to show for a feat like this than bragging rights, spicing-up your journey with a reason or personal mission will give it more meaning.

313. Make a Call from a London Phone Booth

Forget changing into a superhero outfit; you will need to hail the help of a local if you want to pull off this (surprisingly foreign) feat. Pay attention to your instructor when he / she gives you the launch codes for what could easily be an alien aircraft. Fun is optional; if you are a fan of English gangster movies, mimic a cockney accent and see whether it helps or hinders your efforts.

314. Bake Bread

The easiest way to bake bread is to follow the no-knead strategy. With nothing more than a little salt, instant yeast, flour, water, casserole dish and 24 hours, you will have crusty, bubbly bread your friends and family will go bananas over (banana chocolate-chip bread is next). No matter what loaf comes out of your oven, cut a slice and slather it with butter.

315. Eat a Raw Oyster

Aphrodisiac to some; slimy sea creatures to others. If you are of the former camp, you snub your nose at the latter. To each their own.

316. Live in a Different Country

The expat communities in other countries are welcoming, friendly and open to outsiders (so you will never feel like one). Even if you want to 'go native' and never see another person of similar heritage / culture (nor hear the words of your native tongue spoken within earshot ever again) there are 195 countries in the world (the only wildcards are your finances / interests / passions). What climate do you enjoy? What food do you love? What language would you love to speak? What kind of architecture makes you feel at home? Just as there is a monk for every nun, there is a country for every one. Begin with a reconnaissance mission and see what you like.

317. Hike To The Hollywood Sign

As you blaze the trail *"originally blazed by paws, hooves and yucca-thatched moccasins"* up to the more-famous-than-the-film-industry-itself iconic 9 letters, you can gaze beyond *The City of Angels* to the Pacific Ocean (which has no memory, according to Mexican legend) on a clear, smog-free (don't count on it) day.

318. Climb a Mountain

Unless you have already conquered K2, Everest is probably out of question. No problem. Retirement is about enjoyment (you have suffered enough). Do the words 'bunny hill' give you a sense of deep calm and mild serenity? If so, no need to suffer any longer: tackle a guided glacier tour with a bunch of fellow retirees armed with ski poles. Remember: speed (and fear of heights) kills.

319. Watch Baby Turtles Hatch

After hatching and flopping their way to the sea, only 1 in 5,000 sea turtles will live long enough to return to the place they were born and birth the next generation. If you go, don't intrude; turtle moms are protective; they don't need you making life any harder than it already is. Where can you catch a glimpse of reptile nature? Malaysia, Costa Rica, Sri Lanka, Oman, Mexico, Turkey, Mozambique or the Philippines.

320. Visit Every Country in the World

Why would you want to visit 195 countries? Oscar Wilde said *"everything worth knowing cannot be taught"*, and some people feel that everything worth knowing can be learned by traveling. So: if the more you travel, the more you learn, then visiting 195 countries will make you 195 times smarter-in-what-really-matters than someone who has never left their front porch (but life is not a competition).

321. Cuddle a Baby Tiger

In the event you manage to schmooze your way into a furry love sandwich, get it while you can (while they are young) because at the age of about 4 months, they get too big for cuddles (and will let you know it sooner than you can scream for help).

322. Eat Pie

To be fulfilled, fill your life (the space between the crusts) with the nouns you love. Feeling unfulfilled? Darn it if there isn't a pie eating contest within a day's driving distance. By now you are aware that when life has given lemons, lemon meringue pie has always been there (and will continue to be) for you. So go ahead and organize / sponsor / host / emcee a pie party (as a fundraiser for a local charity, of course) and stuff your face with quite possibly the most popular (and versatile) baked dessert on earth.

323. Publish a Cookbook

This takes time, food, energy, friends and/or family, a notebook (or 5), an oven, a kitchen, a dishwasher, a huge grocery shop (or 5) and pounds of patience and love for the food you love. If you are un-daunted, publishing your own cookbook is one of the most rewarding / tasty / exasperating / rich / time-consuming activities you could devote your entire retirement to. But if you love your food and the science / details that make your favorite dish your favorite dish, then this is your life's work.

324. Swim with Sharks

Around since the dawn of underwater civilization, sharks are the ultimate predator. Not especially human-hungry, they are swift, sharp, evolved killers. Given the right circumstances, you are nothing but another swimmingly fishy meal. Opt for the cage if they are bigger than you and you want to live.

325. Buy a Deep Fryer

Is there anything better than fried food? This author would argue (against his girlfriend's better judgement): no. But you may have healthier habits. If this is the case, count yourself lucky. Otherwise, give in to battered Mars bars, french fries, donuts, chicken wings, ice cream, bananas, perogies, corn, fish, bacon, whole turkeys, cookie dough (and anything else you can think of) and just get it over with. You will be much happier. Promise.

326. Sleep on the Beach

After a night of debauchery, there is nothing like falling asleep on the beach. Sleeping bag and tent (or not) it doesn't matter. The point is: sleeping on the beach. Of course, a sound sleep cannot be guaranteed. But what this author *is* promising is an adventurous - possibly romantic - experience (which is what money and time and energy are for).

327. Go on an African Safari

If only lions and tigers and bears evoked oh my's (but tigers and bears don't live in Africa). Instead you will have to settle for seeing elephants, giraffes, leopards, cheetahs, rhinos, buffalos and hippopotami instead. Can you handle it? The more you shell out for this privilege, the more swanky your safari guide / ride / experience will be (safer too).

328. Tour the Galapagos Islands

An archipelago of volcanic islands on the Ecuadorian equator; do you need anything more? Considered one of the most diverse places on the planet to see wildlife that doesn't exist anywhere else, these islands were the inspiration behind Charles Darwin's theory of evolution back in 1835. Explorers of all shapes and sizes are required to hire a guide or join a tour if they wish to find Darwin's ghost (if you find him, have a notebook ready; he may want to expand on his widely-accepted theory).

329. Explore Patagonia

Soaring mountains and jagged glaciers, Patagonia is a hiker's dream. A buffet of hot springs, forests, fjords, bogs, historic fishing villages, breathtaking kayak trips, skiing, llamas and penguins, the southern-most tip of South America shared by Chile and Argentina is best experienced in either the Spring (when the flowers bloom) or in the Fall (when the leaves turn brown, orange and red). The weather is unpredictable all year, so be prepared when you go trudging to the ends of the earth.

330. Walk Around Angkor Wat

A UNESCO World Heritage Center, this temple complex in Cambodia surrounded by a moat used up more stone than the Egyptian pyramids combined. As the largest religious monument in the world, it is Cambodia's most popular tourist destination, so if you are in Southeast Asia, why not swing by?

331. Watch The Wildebeest Migrate

This natural event has been rated as spectacular among those-in-the-know. Each year, more than a million wildebeest, antelope and zebra go clockwise through 2 countries within the Serengeti / Masai Mara ecosystem, all the while getting it on with each other. But your timing has to be just right, or you won't see any furry courting, mating or babies being born (blame it on changing weather patterns).

332. Be a Super Hero

First things first: get yourself a name. Second: an outfit. The more colorful, the better (you want to be seen by drivers / cranes / aircraft / hunters / wild dogs when you are leaping around like a crazy person). At the very least, get some martial arts training and stick to the armaments legal in your state (the last thing you want when heading into a showdown with your arch nemesis is to be detained and disarmed by the real crime fighters).

333. Couch Surf

As you go trekking / exploring / walking / hiking / biking / kayaking / canoeing / skiing / snowshoeing / racing / riding / paddling your way around the planet (or countryside) why not stay with people (in their homes) and soak up some culture while you're at it? If you like people, you will make friends who will give you the inside scoop on local events; take you to the best restaurants; and share their knowledge of the area with you (which will help you feel like a local, not a tourist). Join a hospitality exchange program; sharing meals, stories and experiences with your 'hosts' will be the best part of your trip.

334. Trek Through The Himalayas

You are only as old as you remember you are (or in this case, only as old as your feet). With breath-taking views, friendly people, exotic local cuisine, and other pilgrims on the path, you will fall in love with the Himalayas.

335. Hang with Mountain Gorillas

Gorillas don't age-discriminate (although baby mountain gorillas don't like chameleons and caterpillars for some reason). You're retired, not expired. On the critically-endangered list (found in only 3 places on earth: Uganda, Rwanda, and the Democratic Republic of Congo) if Jane Goodall of chimpanzee fame has been your hero since you were little, you had better hang-ten with these highly-social creatures while you still can.

336. See The Taj Mahal

The real one in India, silly (not the Trump Taj Mahal in Atlantic City that closed its doors in 2016 after years of losing money). Meaning 'Crown of the Palace' this UNESCO World Heritage Site in the city of Agra is universally-recognized as *"the jewel of Muslim art in India and a masterpiece of world heritage"*. Once you acclimatize to sensory-overload, you will fall in love with Indian culture.

337. Binge Watch Netflix

Addictively entertaining (read: soul-sucking), chances are this massively successful media company knows more about you than you do. But don't feel bad; more of your peers than not are getting a kick out of their retirement in front of a screen (if it wasn't Netflix, everyone would be hypnotizing themselves in front of some other rectangular device pulsing with light and sound). Thank goodness some people click on 'documentary' and actually learn something.

338. Perform Card Magic

Sleight of hand is the secret behind card magic (that, and a rigged deck of cards). Direct your audience's attention to where you want them to look (drawing it away from discovering your slick tricks) and before you know it you will be uttering the magic words. No, not 'please' and 'thank you' but rather *"pick a card... any card."*

339. Bird

This author was introduced to the wild world of birding via the cute comedy *The Big Year*, a film celebrating the lengths (and ends of the earth) some enthusiasts will go to see the most species of birds in a single year. All you need is a pair of binoculars (visit your local sporting goods store), a little time (you have a lot) and an interest in the hobby (that some would call a sport).

340. Float in The Dead Sea

Saltier than your mother-in-law, the Dead Sea will suck every bit of moisture from your body. Don't shave or nick yourself before or during your dip (you know what salt does to cuts) and don't fall asleep or stay in too long, or you may shrivel up like a raisin (and you thought lingering in the bubble bath back at the hotel was bad). But it's not all dehydrating: Just lay back, grab a newspaper, and let the sun and salt do their work. Then take a shower. Twice.

341. Defend Yourself

Learn self-defense and you will either find yourself using it (because you expect to) or never needing it (because you are no longer expecting to). If you feel like a victim of circumstances and other nouns, why not prepare for the unexpected (either defending yourself or walking around with confidence). Either way, you win.

342. Backpack Through Europe

Not only for North American college students and Australian kids (people, not goats) on a gap year, stuffing your rucksack with your worldly possessions (everything else safely in storage) and buying a 3-month EuroRail pass will expand your horizons beyond your comfort zone. If you have never left your hometown and didn't get the memo: The earth isn't flat. In fact, it's well-rounded (which is what you will be after a summer sojourn through The Old Country).

343. Get Shipped Across The Pond

Good thing you are not in a rush, because freighter travel is slow travel. Depending on the nationality of your crew, you will be eating like a Northern European (imagine pickled fish, smoked cheese, hard-boiled eggs, cured meat and fresh bread) or a South Sea Pirate (imagine tropical fruit salads, colorful stir-fries with rice and noodles flavored with pungent spices). Writer, reader, documentarian, hobo or solo traveler, after 7 days crossing the deep blue Atlantic, you will not be the same person.

344. Weave The Silk Road

An ancient network of trade routes connecting China to the Mediterranean, you can now join a tour that will transport you along the Silk Road (Silk Route) via camel, private train or bus. Of course you could rough it in your outfitted 4x4 vehicle, or even go by foot. Sounds colorful and unconventional, so get your visas, silk-worm vaccination and go!

345. Catch a Big Fish

Man or woman, deep sea fishing is a thrill. Wrestling your catch into the boat will require the help of your guide (as will also perhaps baiting and casting your rod) but that's what you are paying him for. The experience of fishing a mile or two offshore on a big boat with a bunch of happy (drunk) strangers in search of lunch is an experience you will never forget. Remember: if your catch tastes funny, it's probably a clown fish.

346. Spend Oktoberfest in Germany

It will take you 2 weeks to sober up and remember how much inexpensive German beer you drank; all the best wurst you ate; and the bona fide lederhosen fashion shows you sat through. Of all folk festivals in Bavaria, you will remember the 2 weeks of folk festivities known as Oktoberfest as the most enjoyable fortnight of your life.

347. Raise a Glass To St. Patrick

Most famous for banishing the snakes (read: pagans) from Ireland, everyone kicks off the fun at least a week before March 17th (which like Easter Week or Christmas Week makes for an even more jovial atmosphere across the most magically green-like-you-have-never-seen spot of earth lovingly known around the world as the Emerald Isle).

348. Visit Stonehenge

You don't have to be a druid to appreciate the site built 3,000 years before Christ. When you've had one-too-many green pints of *Guinness* but are hungry for more history / mystery, head for Stonehenge. (Un)fortunately, a knee-high rope fence was built in 1977 to keep out the ne'er-do-wells, though English Heritage still allows access to the stones during equinox and solstice (for those with love and light in their hearts and spells to be cast for the good of all involved).

349. See The Original Fireworks

When was the first time you saw fireworks? It was probably on TV as part of the opening credits to The Wonderful World of Disney. The fireworks go off every night (with special 'spectaculars' on July 4th, New Year's Eve, Hallowe'en, and other special days of the year). Haven't seen them? Everyone (even you) can rouse their inner child from his / her perpetual slumber for one night (or week) of wonder at *"the most magical place on earth."*

350. Capture Uluru

Whether forever in your mind's eye, on film, or simply with your digital camera, capturing the magnificence of Ayers Rock in the Australian Outback will take your breath away. But hope that's all that gets taken away: if your family is in tow, keep a close watch on your newborn grandchild, because the last thing you want is a hungry dingo doing what dingos do.

351. Ride an Elephant

Lumbering through the jungle for an afternoon on the back of this gentle animal is delightful yet exploitative. Activists proclaim *"if you love elephants, don't ride them."* But until these magnificent leather-skinned mammals join the endangered species list, tourists will pay for the pleasure; thus elephant tour guides will continue offering rides. It is up to you to make your own entertainment / ethics decisions.

352. Go For a Stroll Geisha-Style

This is Japan; even men can get away with dolling themselves up like 'professional entertainers'. In the Miyagawa Geisha district of Kyoto, your handlers will dress you up and make you up like a delicate flower and parade you safely through the streets. Be prepared: you will be stared at (but not to worry: your photographer's high-priced commemorative photographs will ensure that living out your fantasy was well worth it).

353. Marvel at The Northern Lights

According to *The Space Weather Prediction Center* of the noble *National Oceanic and Atmospheric Administration*, both Aurora Borealis and Aurora Australis (Southern Lights) *"are the result of electrons colliding with the upper reaches of Earth's atmosphere (protons cause faint and diffuse aurora, usually not easily visible to the human eye)."* Appears not even these geeks can explain why they are so awesome.

354. See a Polar Bear in Churchill

Churchill is 1000 kilometers (620 miles) from Winnipeg, the capital city of Manitoba (and the nearly-uninhabitable-in-winter geographic center of Canada). Yet a close friend of this author recently shared her plans to retire in the said wasteland affectionately known as Manitoo-bad. No need to suffer like her; catch a glimpse of these snow-white bears before your eyes freeze over, and get out while you can.

355. Get a Henna Tattoo in India

A henna artist will mix the dried, powdered pigment of the henna plant with water to temporarily dye (or stain) your skin with decorative designs. Like a baker writing well-wishes on a cake, the 'tattoo' artist adorns your body with the orange paste that when dry, deepens into a reddish-brown color. The only downside is that a henna tattoo is temporary; always fading before you want it to.

356. Go Undercover

Going undercover as a mystery shopper is safer than becoming a law enforcer (you get to pretend to be someone you're not, but you don't risk life and limb infiltrating and taking down an international crime ring). Just as both life and business are games, mystery shopping is one way to play both. But think again: are the companies who retain marketing agencies (who then hire consumer sleuths) simply investing in qualified leads?

357. Exercise

Make sure you read that right: the 357th way to get a kick out of retirement is 'exercise' not 'extra fries'. Walk around the block (or across the country); start jogging once or twice a week; put on a DVD fitness program and stumble along; get a membership at your local recreation center or gym (your choice will depend on not only your fitness level, but also your ability to flirt with the opposite sex). At the very least, get your body moving. Stretch every morning and then try some sit-ups or a few jumping jacks.

358. Soak in a Hot Spring

Whether developed, or deep in the wilds of wherever; natural or not, lay hydrotherapy is a truly healing experience. Better than a hot tub, sliding into an outdoor bath warmed by mineral water bubbling from beneath the surface of the earth will forever be hailed as a stimulating 'clothing optional' adventure.

359. Ride in a Helicopter

If you are big shot, you probably take the big steel bird on your yacht for granted. But that will change the day your luxury yacht sinks in the middle of the ocean and your bird goes down with it (so much for the best helicopter ride of your life). For the rest of us, a ride in a chopper means a lift up to the powder snow, or a scenic sight-see above a National Park.

360. Float in a Hot Air Balloon

For just a few hundred bucks, sailing on the wind high above the ground (but not too high) anywhere from just-above-the-tree-tops to around 2,000 feet is both a terrifying yet sensational way to see the sights. With nothing but hot air between you and Mother Earth, if you can get over your fear of heights, the feeling is beyond exhilarating; the view unforgettable (especially if you catch a glimpse of a few farmer-faked crop circles in the fields below).

361. Snorkel The Great Barrier Reef

This 2,300 kilometer (1,430 mile) reef is the largest living organism on earth; home to 600 types of coral and hundreds of islands, this ecosystem is visible from space. Habitat to turtles, dolphins, starfish, sharks and other colorful creatures, you won't get a kick out of your retirement until you at least swim in nature's orgasm (otherwise known as the more-appropriately named Great Barrier Reef).

362. Walk The Great Wall of China

If you consider 'opportunity cost' (missing out on something by choosing something else) you will have to weigh the benefits of getting a kick out of retirement by walking the 5,500 miles (8,851 kilometers) from Hushan to Jiayuguan Pass. To some this is a journey of a lifetime (to others, it's a model for the wall between the United States and Mexico). What it is to you will depend on your world view.

363. Watch Whales

Orcas (the marine mammals formerly known as killer whales) are spectacular creatures, so if you are ever on the west coast of Canada, this is a must-do. Lucky for you, there are no shortage of whale watching tours eager to guarantee respectful-distance viewings of blow-hole waterworks and big-fin magic acts. Yes, you could visit the Vancouver Aquarium, but it's not the same.

364. Go Storm Watching

Pounding waves, dense fog, gray skies and bundled beach combing through tidal pools are only a few of the reasons to go storm watching. Admittedly most-spectacular on the west coast of Vancouver Island, the nights you spend listening to the rainforest outside your window, curled up by the fire with good food, good wine and good people, is what will make this trip so memorable.

365. Build an Igloo

How can ice and snow keep you warm? They keep the cold wind out and the warm air in (if you have a candle, camp stove or build a small fire). Use a knife, saw, or your hand to cut blocks of snow, then gradually angle and arch them inward to form a dome. Pack the leaks with snow, clear out a sunken living room, and remember to build a door (or no one will ever see your pictures).

366. Visit The Sistine Chapel

Have you ever wondered what is so special about the 16th chapel? And why the other 15 never get any press? Hopefully you haven't. But for those not in-the-know, The Sistine (not sixteenth) Chapel is the Pope's house (until it isn't, which prompts the joke: what do you call a Pope who quits? Ex-Benedict). Apologies: this joke wasn't fair to the finest item ever to hit the brunch menu.

367. Cruise

Is there anything better than eating, drinking, sleeping, swimming, spectating, shopping and gambling? And then doing it all over again the next day? And then again the day after that? And that's only if it's a 3-day cruise. Sign up for a week or more, and you might as well walk the plank. Cruising is a relaxing way to max out your credit card on pleasure and endless debauchery. If you have money to burn, an addictive personality, and time to kill, then you were made to cruise (or cruising was made for you). You decide.

368. Avoid Mona Lisa's Stare

Leonardo da Vinci's 14th century masterpiece depicting Lisa Gherardini is the most visited, best-known, highest-valued, most-parodied painting in the world. Beware: once your eyes meet, she will follow you wherever you go. It's not a conspiracy; it is merely an illusion. Relax. You aren't being followed... Or are you?

369. Visit The Amazon Rainforest

As the largest tropical rainforest in the world, famous for its biodiversity, there must be *something* to see / do / enjoy among the 16,000 different species of tree. Twice the size of India, if jungle birds sing to you from afar (or if you fall asleep fantasizing you are fighting off piranhas gnashing at your toes) go before clearcuts further benefit the cattle industry.

370. Compete in a Bath Tub Race

Held the last weekend in July, the *Nanaimo Bath Tub Race* is the most well-known event of its type. Building your own bath tub racer, or watching wannabe sailors risk life and limb from the shore (or real boat) is a barrel of fun. This annual event will bring a smile to your face when you see the barely-sea-worthy vessels built / decorated in a spirit of whimsy. What's best are the fish and chips and craft beer afterwards. Good thing Seattle is close.

371. Buy a One–Way Ticket

Have you ever gone somewhere without knowing how or when you would come back? A leap of faith, for sure. But when was the last time you leapt into the void of possibility and potential? Adventure awaits you when you step off the metaphorical cliff and jump face-first into the wind. Even better: blindfold yourself and throw a dart at a map. What is life for, other than for experimental adventures with the nouns you love? What's more: they are usually half the price of a return trip, so what are you waiting for?

372. Read The Harry Potter Series

The 7 enormously-popular fantasy novels about a young wizard and his friends are cult treasures. If you have read them, you know why (if you haven't, there is a reason). Can millions of people be wrong? You bet they can. Does magic exist? That's for you to decide.

373. Fly First Class

Let's be honest: first class is not worth the extra "o" on the price tag (unless being sardined among the commoners behind the ironed curtain cramps your style). On a short flight, the added touch is nothing more than a bonus. Though on a long-haul journey the reclining bed, dedicated restroom, personal entertainment system, satellite phone and free champagne might be worth the extra "o".

374. Explore a Shipwreck

There are countless sunken ships sitting there waiting to be explored; some have been waiting for some (any) attention for hundreds of years. Muster some luck and some resources and go uncover some ill-gotten gains left behind by bumbling pirates a century ago. There are millions (if not billions) of dollars worth of ocean floor treasure to be had. Just pick your fellow treasure-hunters wisely or you will be had.

375. Spend a Night in Ice

Weather dependent, an ice hotel is essentially a glorified igloo, a temporary contraption built from blocks of sub-zero ice and snow 'putty'. Depending on your tolerance for cold comfort, the entire operation demands a complete rebuild after the annual meltdown, so enjoy it while it lasts the next time you are in Canada, Finland, Japan, Norway, Romania, Sweden or Switzerland. If you don't have a cuddle partner to keep you warm, pack a hair dryer.

376. Bet on The Kentucky Derby

Considered *"the best 2 minutes in sports"* every year 20 thoroughbred horses get the chance to race in *"the oldest continuously running sports event in the nation"*. It all goes down the first Saturday in May. With odds as high as 74/1, maybe you could win back the small fortune you invested on your flight, hotel, car rental, meals, gratuities and souvenirs.

377. Shave Your Head

Whether in support of cancer research; in honor of your religion; a fashion statement; or just to keep cool in the summer heat, you have your reasons. And no one can take them away from you (except your barber, hairdresser, or spouse with a set of clippers).

378. Let a Floating Lantern Go

Forget George Lucas' industrial enterprise; the people of Thailand know light and magic. On the 12th full moon of the year (usually in November) everyone in their right mind in Southeast Asia at the time visits the Loi Krathong Festival in Bangkok, where candles float down the river on banana-leaf baskets. At the same time up in Chiang Mai, everyone celebrating the *Yi Peng Floating Lantern Festival* fills the night sky with lit lanterns and watches as they float up into the heavens of the southern northern hemisphere. You pick.

379. See a Broadway Musical

Thanks to Richard Rogers and Oscar Hammerstein, Broadway musicals helped to make New York City the cultural capital of the United States (even now, the majority of Broadway performances in the Theater District and Lincoln Center in Midtown Manhattan are musicals). For many actors, Broadway is the last stop on the way to Hollywood (or the farm team during a hiatus) so get a ticket and enjoy the show.

380. Ride a Gondola in Venice

If you are flat-footed, this flat-bottomed Venetian row boat will be your favorite way to float down the backstreets of Venice. This was how everyone used to get around, though nowadays gondoliers ferry supplies around the city and hire themselves out as taxis for tourists, rowing you around in a narrow canoe so you don't have to / get to.

381. Get Your Picture In The Paper

Entertaining / philanthropic / epic exploits are one way to get your picture in the newspaper, but why stop there? A feature interview on your local / regional cable channel is even better. Write a press release promoting your event / do-good deed (or better yet, team-up with a local organization with a PR team on their payroll) and ham it up. When your 15 minutes of fame is over (all good things come to an end) get a copy of your primetime exposure to impress your brilliant, attention-deficit-disordered grandkids for once.

382. Ring in The Year in Times Square

Who doesn't like yelling and screaming and getting drunk and happy and dressing up before cramming themselves into a few square blocks with thousands of other people to celebrate the passing of time on a cold, dark night in an over-populated, polluted city?

383. See a Cirque du Soleil Show

Started by two street performers in 1984, this character-driven contemporary circus is the largest theatrical production company in the world whose mind-blowing events employ 4,000 of the best circus performers from 40 countries (the more we get together, the happier we'll be). FYI: this is performance art at its best.

384. Fly a Drone

A drone is more than a toy, so you can get away with asking Santa for one without feeling guilty. Depending on where you live, un-manned aerial vehicles (UAVs) are governed differently, so check your local listings before you unleash a flyer blizzard on your town; take revenge on your nosy neighbors; launch an aerial photography / videography business; or inadvertently hover over volcanos / craters / glaciers nestled next to military bases. In the case of the latter, shrug and plead ignorance.

385. Take a Pie in The Face

What fun is retirement if you can't take a pie in the face at least once (especially if you think you'd be the last person someone would want to pie)? Even better: bake the pie yourself and give it to someone you love; someone to whom giving you your comeuppance would be as easy as pie.

386. Feed a Giraffe

Want to feed a giraffe, but Africa is too far away? You're not alone. This is why someone took that character Noah literally and rounded up some animals all in one place but thought to charge admission. Some zoos let you pet and feed the critters, so double-check the regulations / hours / presence of the long-necked creatures before you go promising your grandkids (the last thing you need is a bubble-bursted meltdown, especially if giraffes are their favorite animal).

387. Hike The John Muir Trail

Described as America's most famous trail (that took only 46 years to complete), this hike will require a moderate-to-strenuous amount of physical exertion. If you can muster it, you will enjoy relative solitude for the 210 miles (338 kilometers), as fewer than 1,500 people pass through both Yosemite and Sequoia National Parks on their way through the Sierra Nevada mountain range each season. FYI: John Muir was the first president of *The Sierra Club*.

388. Go to a Gay Wedding

If you are lucky to get invited to a gay wedding (you lucky duck) put aside your arrogance-is-ignorance outdated moral judgments and go! If you like that you don't have any gay friends, don't worry: even though *you* are the one going to hell, you still have some time to enjoy yourself before your final destination. Why not at least attend the rainbow reception?

389. Ride a Cab in New York City

Even if this is all you do in NYC, simply the fun, excitement and challenge of hailing one of those yellow steel motorized bumble bees zipping in and out of traffic is an adventure in itself. Need some local advice? A mixture of friendly, surly, helpful and insane, your cab driver is your best friend. Enjoy the sights, because with the most expensive fares in the world, you will be paying for it.

390. Say Mush

The word Mush! soothes the savage sides of the husky-malamute canines bred to taxi you and your gear over tundra so bleak, trails so twisty, and barren so barren, you may get déjà vu of your past life on the planet Hoth (if you don't get frost bite first). But before you go competing in the Yukon Quest, maintain your core temperature by bundling yourself in a blanket and letting your tour guide take the reins for the afternoon.

391. Break Your Bob-Sledding Record

Why anyone would want to slide (read: careen) down an icy slide of ice (read: one wrong move and at least you don't have to go very far to apply ice - or is it heat? to reduce swelling) with nothing more than what appear to be sharpened ice skates between them and the cold, wet, hard surface beneath them is not an activity this author can endorse.

392. Celebrate Mardi Gras

Fat Tuesday; Shrove Tuesday; Carnival; Mardi Gras; it doesn't matter what you call it; what matters is that it's time for one last blow-out before Lent. Over-flowing with pancake syrup, fruit, feathers, flourish, costumes, glow sticks, streamers, balloons and every other dollar-store party accessory you can imagine, you will have a good time no matter where you are in the world (or what you consider as 'fun').

393. Watch a Rocket Launch

Not on TV or *YouTube*; in person. Be flexible, because launches are easily delayed or called off thanks to weather or technical difficulties (even up to a second before launch) so stay flexible when planning your trip to Vandenberg Air Force Base in California; Wallops Flight Facility in Virginia, or to Kennedy Space Center / Cape Canaveral in Florida. Avoid hunting for launch sites in other countries (the last thing you want is to be mistaken for a spy).

394. Go to a Monster Truck Jam

Do you name your vehicle? With names like *Alien Invasion, Bounty Hunter, Monster Mutt Dalmation, Fluffy, Scooby Doo* and *Wild Flower* touring the whole wide world with high-octane entertainment, there is a 1500 horse-powered truck for every personality. Maybe that's why *"the most action-packed live event on four wheels"* is so popular with kids of all ages.

395. Get a Passport

You don't have to be religious to acknowledge saintly wisdom of the ages, or heed poetic advice that resonates with you. Case-in-point: Saint Augustine declared *"the world is a book, and those who don't travel read only a page."* Nowadays you need a passport if you want to go anywhere truly interesting, so get yourself one of these little pocket-sized booklets in your possession and keep it up-to-date so you can leap into the wind going by.

396. Get Into or Onto a Hall or Wall of Fame

According to some, the 3 elements of happiness are: 1) having someone to love; 2) having something to do; and 3) having something to look forward to. So if your heart whispers (or screams) *Hall* or *Wall of Fame*, why not go after the lifetime achievement award from your local community association or sports organization?

397. Make Chocolate

If the 555 ways to get a kick out of retirement are in a league of their own, chocolate is the commissioner of the entire organization. When all you need to transcend your troubles are cocoa beans, cocoa butter, lecithin and a sweetener of your choice, how you transform these simple ingredients into tastebud-tantalizing confections that melt in your mouth is up to you.

398. Smash Plates in Greece

The Greeks say all the fun began when a wealthy family invited a poorer family over for dinner, and when supper was over, invited them to smash their plates to prove that friendship was more important to them than a display of wealth. Or maybe (like most people) they simply didn't want to do the dishes. If you can't get to the stunning Greek islands, at least go to a big fat Greek wedding.

399. Eat Paella in Spain

If you like food, you will love paella. Saffron rice, chicken, chorizo, prawns, mussels, clams and veggies, this popular Valencian dish will have you ditching your return ticket and typing 'how to emigrate to Spain' into *Google* before your waiter returns. Surrounded with Spanish architecture and atmosphere, you may just want to end it all right there in culinary heaven. It would make a great last meal.

400. Smoke a Cigar in Cuba

Cuba used to be close, but no cigar. Now it's easy. Just as there are 6 different types of cigar (Corona, Pyramid, Torpedo, Perfecto, Panatela, Culebra) there are 6 steps to enjoying one. #1. Choose the cigar. #2. Store the cigar. #3. Cut the cigar. #4. Light the cigar. #5. Smoke the cigar. #6. Put out the cigar. For best results, enlist the help of a local aficionado or other seasoned stogie smoker.

401. Change Your Life

Whatever this means to you now (or has meant to you throughout your life) these 3 words tend to provoke thoughts and feelings that either freeze you in Han Solo-approved *carbonite*, or light the fire of possibility and inspire you to think outside the box, challenge yourself and maybe take a risk. If you get scared, go snail-slow: one day / hour / minute / second at a time. What is the worst that can happen?

402. Snowshoe Up a Mountain

Snowshoes are cheaper to rent than skis or a snowboard (and safer and easier to get the hang of too). Mountains come in all shapes and sizes (ant hills are mountains to ants). Pack a thermos of hot chocolate, tea or coffee and spike it with your favorite warming liquor; plan on fondue at the lodge following your excursion and you have the recipe for good times walking in a winter wonderland.

403. Smile

If you are unfortunate enough to have 'resting bitch face' obviously you need to smile more often (at least so people would treat you differently). But maybe you like looking like the feline internet star *Tardar Sauce*. Apparently something *Grumpy Cat* (her code name) hasn't learned is that you can trick your brain into thinking you are happy by pretending to smile. But if you are reading this book, you have a sense of humor, so you have nothing to worry about. Turn that frown upside down.

404. Go Over Niagara Falls

If you can't get your hands on an old wooden barrel, don't even begin to plan your death-defying tumble over the falls, or else you will turn to fish food long before *The Little Mermaid* rescues your dumb ass from the wreckage that was your attempt at life. Instead, peer over the edge like all the other tourists from behind the child-proof railing.

405. Marvel at The Human Body

You can figuratively peel back the layers of your body like an onion skin at the world-renowned *Body Worlds* exhibit. Touring the world and showcasing our fascinating human anatomy via plastic models, the Body Worlds exhibit may be the nail in the coffin (so to speak) as they actively seek donations (arms, legs, etc.) for their newest displays. But think twice if you are private person, because after 'plastination' everyone will be able to see right through you.

406. Freeze Your Ass Off

The ocean in winter is no longer just for penguins and polar bears. Even if you feel more like a seal, joining in the annual *Polar Bear Swim* (plunge is more accurate) is not only a great team-building exercise, but also (and more importantly) a socially-acceptable excuse to get hammered afterwards. Bring a blanket to ward off looming hypothermia.

407. Kiss Under The Mistletoe

The most wonderful time of the year isn't Christmas; it's kissing your sweetheart under the parasitic plant that depends on other plants for survival. No matter how alone and desperate you are the rest of the year, the season of giving is your opportunity to pop a breath mint, pucker up, and casually loiter around the mistletoe waiting for your next victim like you were a venus fly trap. Suggest it to the host if they invite you back next year.

408. Let Someone Feed You Peeled Grapes

Whatever you do, don't imagine said someone is feeding you slippery 'eyeballs' like that one Hallowe'en party where you were blindfolded by well-meaning adults and convinced the spaghetti and meatballs you were easing your hand into wasn't spaghetti and meatballs, but the insides of a mummy's tummy instead. Damn wet tortilla skin and dried apricot ears!

409. See a Marriage Counsellor

When your bond with your spouse is evaporating quicker than water in the dessert, seeing a marriage counsellor can help (though only if you both make an effort, obviously). Hindsight (like perfect vision) is 20-20, so if there is a next time, try marriage counseling *before* you tie the knot. An ounce of prevention is worth a pound of cure, divorce lawyers say.

410. Become a Marriage Counsellor

If your marriage as successful (and others agree) and you haven't already hung your shingle out advertising your methods of happy co-habitation, why not give it a go? You are probably already counseling your friends, but what do you get in return? Empty tissue boxes, wine bottles and rinsed ice cream tubs filling up your recycling bin. Seriously: saving marriages is essential to the health, wealth and happiness of our entire society.

411. Go on a Second Honeymoon

How was the first? Where did you go? What did you do? Do you even remember? Or were you both too drunk on love and booze? Regardless of how long ago you partied like only newly weds party, it's never too early or too late to do it again. If your best man and maid of honor are still around, invite them along (and don't forget the now-grown-up single flower girl who will blaze her way to the bouquet as she eyes-up the now-grown-up ring-bearer).

412. Get Naked Under Water

Skinny dipping is fun, flirtatious, taboo and just what you need to do if it's been a while since you had any racy summertime fun up at the cottage or in your private hot tub). If you're shy, get undressed in the dark and slip into the bubbling bath or glass-surfaced lake when no one is looking (if you're not, you know what you're doing).

413. Learn to Ballroom Dance

An elderly fellow once confided in this author that the biggest regret of his life was not learning how to dance. He lamented how he was surrounded with lovely ladies his entire life, yet never swept the damsels off their feet, whisking them away into a wonderland of movement to music. Married for 50 years, he was a big flirt, convinced this form of intimacy was the secret to having one's cake and eating it too.

414. Join The Mile High Club

Ever gazed into a lover's eyes at 35,000 feet? Ever kissed while cruising at 500 miles per hour? Holding hands during take-off is one thing; creeping into a 2x2 closet-of-a-bathroom and getting it on while it's minus 70 outside is another. Membership is free, so ignore the fasten-your-seat-belt sign and join the most elite club on earth.

415. Get Awoken with a Kiss

If you are single, you can always buy a blow-up doll. They won't kiss back, but you have an imagination, right? If you are lucky, you have a sweetie to keep you warm at night. Wake him / her up with a kiss tomorrow morning. Do this often enough and he / she might eventually get the hint and return the favor.

416. Send Flowers for No Reason

Who doesn't like flowers? And for no reason? Screw Valentine's Day; passionate acts-of-florist are a welcome surprise any time of the year. No one knows what has been stressing your random victim out lately (except for them). Every wants love and attention (and flowers deliver) so send a bouquet to a perfectly good stranger and imagine the delight your simple gesture of kindness will bring to someone other than yourself for once.

417. Lock Up Your Love

You could take this a few different ways, but in this instance 'Lock Up Your Love' refers to locking a padlock to the Love Lock Bridge and throwing away the key. Caveat: to enjoy this 417th way to get a kick out of retirement, you probably need to be in Paris. Now if you are romantically inclined, you will have either already symbolically sealed the fate of your mutual love to the famous bridge, or you had better surprise your hubby before it's too late and they go to the City of Love without you.

418. Leave a Note For a Stranger

What would you love to read on an attractively-decorated note you find on the bus stop or in a shopping basket? What words strung together in a poetic or sincere way would melt your heart / inspire you / encourage you to not give up? Once you figure it out what resides in the collective cockles of all humanity, share your warm fuzzies with the world.

419. Slow Dance in The Kitchen

If you and the companion in your kitchen are nothing more than *"strangers in the night exchanging glances"* you may need to find someone more willing-and-able to slow dance in the kitchen with you. But before you throw the big baby out with the bath water, put on your favorite song and see what happens. Then again, if you have two left feet, there is no hope for you. Ever. Sorry.

420. Masquerade

Oscar Wilde's brilliant observation *"give someone a mask and they will show their true face"* is a free pass to express yourself the 364 other days of the year you can't dress up Hallowe'en-style. Masquerade balls are elegant, sensuous, sophisticated gatherings where people parade around in colorful costumes and malevolent-looking masks designed to disguise their true selves (but now you know the truth).

421. Rip Someone's Clothes Off

It's more fun if you imagine you are on a movie set surrounded with cast and crew while you fake a make-out or full-on love-fest. If you can pull this off, you are an A-List actor worthy of the silver screen (you shouldn't be reading a book on how to get a kick out of retirement). Go take some acting or improv classes and spend the rest of your life perfecting your craft and entertaining the rest of us. Go!

422. Visit The Louvre

The second-largest (and most-famous) museum in the world was once a royal palace. When the first King Francis bought the Mona Lisa in the 16th Century, he established the Louvre as his private are collection. With over one million works of art (35,000 of which are on display) you won't be bored. Oh yeah, and it's in Europe (that continent packed with history, culture, architecture and adventure).

423. Ride in a Glass Bottomed Boat

The Little Mermaid's crabby friend Sebastian knew what he was bubbling about when he proclaimed his (biased) views of life in the deep blue yonder with the lyrics *"Under the sea. Under the sea. Darling it's better down where it's wetter. Take it from me."* The next best thing to scuba diving and snorkeling, who knows what you may catch a glimpse of from the comfort of your glass-bottomed vessel.

424. Meet Someone in Cyberspace

Internet dating, social media websites and comment boxes make connecting with other people online easier than striking up a conversation about the weather with a stranger standing in line next to you at the grocery store. Thanks to the inter-webs, shy people with the ability to express themselves have it easy. The only downside? Reality is never as rosy. So when you meet in person, meet in a public place.

425. Have Sex on a Pool Table

There are more comfortable places (both in and outside of the bedroom) to get it on with someone you like. Pool tables just hold a unique fascination (like sex in a public park holds for others). Whatever your favored flavor of lube or edible panties, this way to get a kick out of retirement is meant to add a swirl of butterscotch ripple or rum-raisin to your vanilla sex life. Just don't sink the 8-ball.

426. Be Happy

Forget getting a kick out of your retirement; why not enjoy every aspect of your life? From now on, instead of complaining about the nouns that seem hell-bent on taking you home with them, you would be wise to remember: *"For general peace of mind, refrain as General Manager of the Universe."* Accepting things as they are (instead of how you think they should be) is the secret to happiness.

427. Give Someone a Diamond

Ear rings; finger rings; necklaces; pendants. It doesn't really matter (unless it does to them, in which case you are hereby advised to rethink your bestowal of such an expensive token of appreciation on someone with such high expectations). In the rare instance the recipient of your physical proclamation of adoration *is* worthy of such an extravagant gift, nothing says *"I love you"* like 3 months of pension payments.

428. Be a Secret Admirer

It's only secret if the person doesn't know it's from you. If you wear your heart on your sleeve and can't help but proudly gush about your sly solicitations, you might as well give up now and get someone else to do the wooing for you. But don't worry you sensitive soul; all is not lost. At the very least, you can take solace in the saying *"practice makes perfect."*

429. Get Down on One Knee

Whether your knee is 'bum', replaced, or in its original packaging, retirement may have you professing your undying love and devotion (for better or for worse) and yearning tie the knot with that hunk or honey you met on the beach last time you were in Mexico. Yes, you have lived and loved more than most, so good for you for falling in love-struck love and being so eager for one more kick at the can.

430. Give Someone a Hickey

Make your mark, but don't puncture the skin and drain them of their vital life juice, unless your love for your 'victim' is so undying that you wish to condemn them to everlasting life as an undead, no-reflection, garlic-fearing plasma-sucker for all eternity. FYI: marking your territory like this only lasts a week (but it's better than peeing on them). So take it easy Vlad and make it look like a bruise.

431. Go Dumpster Diving

The volume of food that goes in the trash is shameful. 20 pound bags of onions, boxes of donuts, grapefruits, pre-packaged sushi, bricks of cheese, televisions, furniture, sporting equipment; it's a veritable goldmine for dumpster-divers. So stake out the freshest loot; use a step ladder; pile up the garbage to get out; bring a few reusable bags; don't wear your best clothes; and be prepared for scornful looks. Who cares. It was free. Share the wealth and go back tomorrow.

432. Discover Machu Picchu

Peru's most popular tourist attraction, visiting the UNESCO Lost City of the Incas is neither cheap nor easy. Begin your adventure in Cusco and take the train (booked as far in advance as possible). Be sure to acclimatize yourself as you go, because the last thing you want is to become an ancient relic yourself (unless cryopreservation seems like the way to go).

433. Ask a Stranger on a Date

If the stranger is single (and doesn't find you repulsive) you can break the ice with: *"I'm on my way to [fill in the blank]. Would you like to come along?"* If they don't get the subtle yet direct hint, act like you were joking and say *"That's okay. I guess I will have to take my husband / wife instead."* On the flip side, if a stranger asks you out (and they seem safe and fun) go with your gut and go for it. Caveat: as in all things, use your best judgement.

434. Get Lost in a Corn Maze

Take a cell phone or a friend along (or both) because the last thing you want is the theme to the *Children of the Corn* movie getting in your head and refusing to leave (like you won't be, if these fictitious demonic children get you before you find your way to the exit). Labyrinths and mazes of any kind are for rats, not humans. Prone to anxiety attacks? Don't go near a haunted corn maze in October.

435. Take a Pole Dancing Class

According to pop culture media, the only goal of some parents is to 'keep their daughter off the pole'. But what if you were a 'good girl' (or boy) your whole life and want to break your moral-coded chains and live a little? This *is* a book about getting a kick out of retirement, after all. Whether you are an aspiring cougar or not, do your own 'leg' work to find a class before the only pole in your life is the safety bar in the bath tub.

436. Go to a Kink / Fetish Party

What deep dark shadows lurk beneath your prim-and-proper conservative façade? There is no time like the present to let your inner animal out of his / her cage (especially if you harbor un-yet-realized sexual fantasies). Entrance into the kink community is often via cute-and-cuddly-sounding 'Strawberry Kink' parties (and there is nothing scary about a strawberry).

437. Play with a Ouija Board

No matter how aloof or reckless you are, evoking (or provoking) contact with the spirit world is best left to professionals. If you are one, you know why. On the other hand, if you just can't enough of your long-lost loved ones, this is a great way to keep the conversation going long after they've left the material plane and cancelled their long distance phone plan.

438. Sleep Somewhere Haunted

Why would you want to sleep somewhere haunted? Because you are either a ghostbuster obsessed with capturing / recording / proving paranormal activity and debunking all the myths and mysteries once-and-for-all, or you thrive on fear and face it at every chance you get. If the latter is true, you have probably been getting your kicks all your life, so put this book down and get back to it.

439. Ride in a Tuk–Tuk

Tuk-Tuks (putt-putts) are motorized rickshaws produced in (and thus popular in) Thailand. But the fun doesn't stop in Southeast Asia or India (where you can get a ride for less than the cost of opening the door of a taxi in North America). Even though these 3-wheeled lawnmowers with seats have put-putted their way all the way Iceland, the quality of your experience will always hinge (sometimes literally) on the mood of your driver, the mood of the traffic, the distance you are traveling, and the time of day.

440. Tame a Wild Animal

Although not without its benefits, do not try to instill new behavior in your wayward spouse in hopes they will become an obedient, house-trained pet (foxes on the other hand seem ripe for domestication, but good luck getting them to listen to your problems, take out the trash, or do the dishes).

441. Own a Pair of Cowboy Boots

Before you make Clint Eastwood's day and trot out to the nearest western outfitter, remember The Cowboy Creed: Just because you fill the boots doesn't mean you can walk in them. Pioneer, bull rider, gunslinger or mountain man / woman; if you like salad, round 'em up and move 'em out, because if you wear cowboy clothes, you are ranch dressing.

442. Try Marijuana in Jamaica

The minute you get off the plane, you will be offered ganja. If not (and you have always wondered why people like that song called reggae) ask a cab driver or someone at your hotel to hook you up. As the best ganja in the world is not technically legal, the worst-case scenario (bust) will involve a fine, so do your due diligence before engaging in any activity promoted in this book and you will get more than your share of kicks out of retirement for years to come.

443. See a Sumo Wrestling Match

Are you fat and happy, and want more role models in your life? Go to Japan. Sumo wrestlers eagerly pack in 4,000 calories of a traditional meat-and-veggie stew called *chanko-nabe* before stepping into the ring and either ousting their opponent from the circle or forcing them to touch the ground with any body part but their feet. The matches often last only a few seconds, so don't get drunk on saki, pass out, and miss all the fun.

444. Model in a Fashion Show

Could you prowl (or claw) your way down the catwalk like a furry feline? Whether you want to model hair, clothing, shoes or accessories, opportunities abound (even for 'mature' models with 'life experience'). Check your local listings (or host / produce / star in your own show) if you want to flaunt what you got.

445. Sleep Naked

The higher the thread count, the higher the quality (and the higher the quality your sheets, the better your sleep). Pima cotton, cotton percale and silk are the best, though rolling around by yourself (or with someone else) between any set of sheets with a 250+ thread count with no pesky clothing getting in the way will ensure you never wear pajamas again.

446. Make a Fool of Yourself

How often must you heed this unsolicited advice? Whenever you get too serious / worried / stressed / anxious / afraid / angry complacent / dictatorial / overwhelmed. The solution is simple (if not revolutionary): do something out of the ordinary (to heck with what others think) and have more fun. The best part of laughter ain't the medicine; foolery often attracts onlookers whose laughter will be contagious. The sooner you learn to giggle at your goofy self, the easier life will seem.

447. Try a Sensory Deprivation Tank

Called *"a spiritual and emotional detox"*, floating in body-temperature salt water loaded with epsom salts in a floatation chamber has been an ebbing-and-flowing alternative health craze since 1954. Buoying yourself in this solution is like being back in the womb; with purported benefits including reduced cortisol (stress hormone) levels, only one question remains: where is the nearest isolation tank?

448. Start (and Win) a Food Fight

First of all: ensure a steady supply of your chosen weapon(s): Apple sauce, mashed potatoes, pudding, scrambled eggs and whipped cream are favorites. Second: limit your enemy's supply (or access to) equally-messy weaponry (if possible). Third: position yourself near the fridge (just in case you need to reload). The rest will depend on the number of combatants involved and everyone's capacity for edible mayhem.

449. Host a Cuddle Party

Mutually-consenting adults engaging in non-sexual cuddling sessions (in public and in private) is no surprise when few people get their recommended daily intake of physical touch. Theories like *"four hugs a day for survival; eight for maintenance; and twelve for growth"* is the driving force in the cuddle movement that welcomes both cuddlers and cuddlees. So sign up today and get the squeeze you need.

450. Jump Into a Pool of Jello

You need a pool of jello before you can jump into one, so get dissolving. And you may need some qualified help, so plan ahead. Where do you get your hands on your much-needed supplies? Try the home supply store for the kiddie pool, and the bulk store for the flavored gelatin powder? jello. When you're ready, encourage everyone to slip into their birthday suit; everyone will have way more fun.

451. Take a Pin-Up Style Photo

Pin-up girls have been enchanting us since the 1940's. Want to emulate their natural beauty and confidence? Cruise the thrift and vintage shops for your wardrobe; give yourself a beauty mark; perfect your pout; wriggle into a corset; do your hair and make-up; and then find a professional photographer who can also add some digital effects to make your photos look even more authentic.

452. Participate in a Flash Mob

Have you ever been surprised by a group of people (seemingly randomly) breaking out into song and dance in the middle of the shopping mall? Want to join in the fun? Just show up for practice (in costume, if applicable) and let it all out. Come next October, find the people who make things happen so you can indulge your taste for human flesh and let your inner zombie out recreating Michael Jackson's *Thriller* music video in a seemingly random public place.

453. Eat a Bug

Screw up your nose and give yourself more wrinkles or dig in. Protein-packed bugs are a treat. Crunchy, gooey, squishy, spicy; take your pick (like 2 billion people do every day). How will you know unless you try it? Chances are: deep-fried ants and chocolate-covered spiders will have you trumpeting the cause. But don't go around telling everyone that you are an 'insectivore' just yet. People don't like what they don't understand.

454. Give or Get Oral Sex

As a giver or a receiver of fellatio and/or cunnilingus, you are likely hip to the subject (so this kick is for virgin lips). First of all, there is nothing to be afraid of. Whether number 454 is a reminder or a prompt, ask your partner what they like; explore their body; and revel in your sex life. Happy wife = Happy life. Happy spouse = Happy house.

455. Pay a Stranger's Restaurant Bill

How would you feel if when you asked for the bill the next time you are out on the town the server informed you that your late breakfast / lunch / dinner / round of drinks had been paid for in full by a well-meaning soul who wanted to fund your antics (or apologize for theirs?) What would have to happen (positive or negative) for *you* to even consider doing something like that?

456. Go on a Vision Quest

Instead of embarking on a self-guided adventure where you wake up no wiser from the experience, let a trained shaman lead you into, through, and out of a mystical experience that more-often-than-not results in a greater understanding of both your life and your place in it. What is the nature of reality? What does it all mean? *The Little Prince* said *"It is only with the heart that one can see rightly. What is most important is invisible to the eye."*

457. Experience an Earthquake

The earth is moving, shaking and settling daily; not even scientists can tell you the next time a human settlement will be leveled by the forces of nature. Want better odds? Spend more time on a fault line and wait it out like everyone else. Finally, lighting up the Richter Scale is not a requirement; a gentle rock 'n' roll rumble will qualify. The real question is: are you prepared for The Big One?

458. Milk a Cow

Oh the fresh barn air; 'mucking out' said barn; feeding and tending the moos; building and fixing what needs to be built and fixed; fresh milk, butter, eggs, cheese, yogurt, meat and vegetables. If you didn't grow up on a farm, there is a farmer nearby (with a cow nearby) needing milking (it happens twice a day, 365 days a year). This unique experience will be most rewarding if the farmer knows how to cook and invites you for lunch.

459. Grow a Chia Pet

Ch-ch-ch-chia! This animal-shaped clay pot (for lack of a better description) growing (what looks like) hair or fur is entertaining for about 30 seconds. But it's better than watching another commercial. Mix up a chia seed paste, plaster it on your terracotta friend and wait a few weeks for nature to do its thing. It's easy (grass doesn't strain to grow) and snail-slow fun for the whole family. When you take your chia seed pet for a walk, make sure everyone on social media knows about it.

460. Get a Vanity License Plate

Vanity plates are like domain names (both allow someone to own a word or number) but some take it too far: in Saudi Arabia, the number 5 license plate sold for US$6.8 million. Don't feel the need to auction off your grandkids so as to doth your ride with a creative moniker (unless availability and local rules otherwise limit your options).

461. Get Honey from a Beehive

Where would you bee without bees? You wouldn't bee. Responsible for pollinating fruit and vegetable plants, domesticated honey bees gather nectar and store it in their wax honeycomb nests to feed every bee in the colony. Remember: they can smell fear, so when you pillage their village like *Winnie The Pooh*, put on the sting-proof suit and don't forget the billowed smoker.

462. Go Under The Knife

Like black-and-white American foreign policy, you are either for (or against) elective cosmetic surgery. What is so bad about a little nip-and-tuck? Nothing, except most patients don't know when to stop. Look at the entertainment industry: aging movie stars end up (ironically) looking like the very thing they feared becoming: scary monsters. But that won't happen to you, because you *"know when to fold 'em."*

463. Make a Pornographic Video

'Regular' couples regularly venture into the uncharted territory beckoning most people (those with spice in their cupboards / closets). As a bedroom media mogul, you don't need fancy equipment, props or scripts (though all will improve your production value). You also don't need any crew except you and your co-star (unless you do; that's up to you). Ready? Turn down the lights. Turn on the camera. Action!

464. Chat with a Parrot

The more enthusiastic you are, the quicker your bird will learn. Start with (obviously) *"hello"* and *"goodbye"*; inform them of what you're doing, ask them questions, and have a conversation. The best 'talkers' are African Grey Parrots, Amazon Parrots and Umbrella Cockatoos. But stay away from lovebirds (they will mostly scream at you).

465. Give an Anonymous Tip

Not deterred by the crime drama plot-driver phrase *"snitches get stitches"?* Why not become a police informant? What have you got to lose? Forget ratting out the local meth lab / crack house / grow-op next door (the last thing you want is to misinterpret an innocent look the next time you take Fluffy for a walk and rush home to board up your windows). Same goes for out-ing a cheater. But if you can't help yourself, tread lightly, super hero.

466. Get a Ride in a Police Car

There are 2 ways to get a ride in a police car (and 2 places to sit, depending on how you managed to get a ride). The first is obvious: be an idiot and do something idiotic (ensuring you get to sit in the back like a chauffeured rock star). Second: make a friend on the force and ride shotgun on a routine patrol (no, chances are you won't get to wear a bullet proof vest).

467. Perform Stand-Up Comedy

Could you wing-it? Pick on someone and make the butt of your entire set? Or would you need hours of rehearsal and still have to take recipe cards on stage with you? Speaking in public strikes fear into most hearts; pulling off a stand-up comedy routine takes enormous courage (and/or foolishness). Props to you if you dream of making people laugh and have the guts to do it semi-professionally. Everyone began at Amateur Night.

468. Do Tequila Shots in Mexico

You can't walk down a street in a tourist town in Mexico without being invited to try-before-you-buy-any-flavor-of-tequila-you-can-imagine by friendly shop keepers of all ages. Always more expensive than a DIY drink fest back at the swim-up bar (but far from authentic), if you are passionate about Mexico's most popular export, try them all, and drink plenty of water before bed (but not from the pool).

469. Play with Spray Paint

There are as many ways to play with spray paint as there are colors of the toxic stuff. Graffiti artist / folk artist / construction worker / forester / hooligan / auto body technician; you don't need a fancy (or homely) title to do what you gotta get done. Marking property lines, creating murals, vandalizing public property or redecorating; spray paint ain't as harmful to the environment as it used to be, so go for the gold (silver is nice too).

470. Hitch a Ride

If you have never hitch-hiked, you are missing out on (terrifying) adventure. Risky (yet life-saving when you need a lift to the nearest gas station) hitching a ride with a stranger is a thrill. For those uniquely interested in the environmentally-friendly aspects of this transportation option, trusted car-sharing networks review / vet your driver before you get it, so arriving in one piece is possible.

471. Write Your Memoirs

If you are curious about your grandparents, there is a good chance your grandchildren will be curious about you. Why disappoint them? Your life's work is incomplete until you have told your story, yet no one knows your story like you do (nor can they tell it as you can). Memories pile up like boxes of unsorted photos, so why not give your loved ones the gift of a lifetime?

472. Spike Your Hair

Give yourself a mohawk or simply spike your hair with various gel / mousse / spray / mud / wax hair products. As popular nowadays as concocting oil-and-egg hair conditioner was in ancient Egypt, frizz-fighting, follicle-friendly fashion resembling ski jumps, jagged mountain ranges, and choppy water is how both men and women have been expressing their uniqueness for ages. Live a little.

473. Perform in a Burlesque Show

The word burlesque comes from the Italian word 'burlesco' which comes from the Italian word 'burla' (both mean joke, mockery or ridicule). As such, burlesque shows are dramatic / musical / literary events that poke fun at serious subjects. Funny, sexy, political and colorful, anything goes. If you are inclined to enjoy theatre performance, a burlesque show is the next step.

474. Play an April Fool's Joke

As long as you don't cause physical or emotional harm, or destroy someone's property, all else is fair game. Try assaulting someone's tastebuds with caramel onions, or hide plastic bugs in the vegetable aisle at the grocery store. You could put up a 'For Sale' sign in your front yard, or undo the shampoo bottle and cover the cap with plastic wrap. Just because you are a mature adult doesn't mean you have to act like one.

475. Hold a Snake

If the snake is a big snake, you will need some help (heck, even if the snake is small and you haven't held one before you had better get a second set of hands). #1. Wash your hands. #2. Let the snake know you're going to pick it up. #3. Avoid sudden movements. #4. Keep the meet-and-greet short. #5. Put it back where it belongs. #5. Wash your hands again. If the snake starts to wrap itself around your neck and squeeze, don't give up.

476. Place a Bet with a Bookie

You are not legally allowed to bet on the outcome of a sporting event in Nevada, Oregon, Delaware or Montana, so go to Europe where 'bookmaking (the profession of accepting sports wagers) is not criminalized but rather regulated for the benefit of all concerned (mostly the regulators). Wherever you feel like throwing your money away: *"Know your limit. Play within it."*

477. Sunbathe Topless

Why are breasts banned from the beach when hairy chests (attractive or not) run rampant along the shorelines, public parks and backyards of America? Didn't Europeans in search of a better life flee the puritanical religious dictates of their oppressors centuries ago for a right such as this? If returning to the motherland is out of the question (and you just want get an even tan for once) find a nude beach nearby. None? Move to California.

478. Racquetball

If you thrive on adrenaline, no sport will get your heart racing more than bouncing off the walls like a racquetball. If you have never stepped foot in a court, consider a lesson (or five) first so you don't end up with a mild concussion or take after John Candy in the movie *Splash*.

479. Play Ping Pong / Table Tennis

If you listen hard (and/or have a vivid imagination) the back-and-forth sounds like 'ping' and 'pong'. Onomatopoeia aside, is there a more engaging sport for the mind and body? Fun for the whole family, you could easily spend the rest of your life becoming the neighborhood champion (the *Jedi Mind Trick* will give you the upper hand).

480. Buy Land on The Moon

NASA wants to build a base on The Big Cheese, but according to the *Outer Space Treaty* that went into effect in 1967, no one owns the moon (so you can't stake your claim and squat on some lunar land anytime soon). Don't believe anyone who says you can (unless you are one of those slick moon-oil salespeople yourself, in which case, don't let your customers read this; the last thing you need is educated prospects). On the other hand, you could start and run a non-profit.

481. Get Branded

Why anyone would get branded is beyond this author's limited comprehension. Regardless, searing one's soft, sensitive skin with with a near-molten-hot flaming cattle iron is definitely one way to get a kick out of retirement. Rest assured, you will be kicking like a bucking bronco (if not braying like a donkey) if you opt for this temporary experience with a permanent payoff.

482. Serenade Someone Special

What if you are neither a trained vocalist nor a virtuoso instrumentalist? Fear not; you can still soothe your savage love beast with music (just don't expect a standing ovation (or the door/window to stay open for long). But don't let anyone (especially this author) discourage you. Sing your song to the one you love and they will be forever yours.

483. Learn To Twirl Nipple Tassels

You can find them at any adult sex shop (except where adult supply stores don't exist). However, if you are reading this book, you are not deterred. Kind of like learning to hula hoop, getting your nipple tassels to spin in sync with (or in opposition to) each other takes practice. But once you have trained them, it's like riding a bike: muscle memory takes over and you have the skill for life. Youth leadership programs have nothing on a life skill like this.

484. Create Your Own Board Game

All you need is a little imagination (you have one of those). Like an alchemist, dream it up and make it. Create an engaging story and theme / likable characters / an objective. Now draw / sketch it all out and fabricate the board and pieces. Then find an agent, lawyer and publisher who will schmooze and work with a distributor and manufacturer to release your game to the world... Or just keep it to yourself.

485. Enjoy a Dose of Valium

Whether you need to switch gears and calm down (or you just like recreational drugs) the benefits and side-effects of *diazepam* are the same. The best-selling drug in the 1970's is still used to treat anxiety, seizures and (the unimaginable) restless leg syndrome (poor twitchy souls). Cheap and effective, it's easy to get addicted. So don't.

486. Have a Threesome

Hi, Thursday. I'm Friday. Wanna come over Saturday and have a Sunday? If they answer affirmatively, make sure your significant other is at least a bit into it. Better yet, decide together beforehand (you don't want any more surprises, and neither do they). The biggest obstacle to polyamory is jealousy, so as long as everyone gets a turn, all will be well. There are some good books on the subject (and a supportive community) if you're serious.

487. Instigate a Riot

Wait until the night of the big game and wear the other team's jersey down to the bar. You *do* have a few in the closet just for riot instigation, don't you? If you really want to get a kick (and a few punches) out of retirement, act like a European football hooligan and chant some provocative mockery throughout the evening so when push comes to shove (as it will) you won't kick the can with your song still inside you.

488. Open a Beer with Your Teeth

If you still have your teeth, what better way to get rid of them? Showing off like a cocky jack-ass never ends well (as you may remember). Still, if you haven't matured past the age of majority and still have something to prove, at least get the illusion right: Pop the top and break the seal when no one is looking, then quickly put it back on and get on with the show, David Copperfield.

489. Try Laughing Gas

Nitrous oxide is sweet and tasty, making it even more enjoyable. And it gets even better: it's cheap, legal, relatively harmless and available online (no surprise it's the 7th most popular drug in the world). Regardless of how negligent you have been with your flossing routine, you can only giggle your troubles away for so long because when it's time to pay your bill, the dentist always gets the last laugh.

490. Go Outside In Your Pajamas

Taking out the trash; walking the dog; gardening; washing the car; going fishing; you can get away with just about anything but going to work (unless you work from home). Going outside in your pajamas is not just a fashion statement; it's a moral standing that was originally meant for lying down. What will your neighbors think? Who cares: they are more worried about what you think of them all dressed up pretending they have a purpose.

491. Get Elected

Do you have something to say? Do people listen when you say it? Are you a leader with strong civic values? Do you have two deep pockets, or access to them? If you answered yes to most (if not all) of the above questions you are fit for community / regional / national leadership (but you know this already). When is the next election in your club / community group / town / city / state / country? Get your beliefs on the bill and rally the support you need to shape the future of those you want to serve.

492. Donate Your Hair

Grow 10 inches end-to-end before you decide to cut your bob and help a cancer patient. Wash and dry your locks; tie it all in a ponytail or braid; pop your mane in a plastic bag; put it in a big envelope and mail it off. FYI: The demand for hair is as high as the need for other secondhand bodily organs, donor.

493. Speak to a Large Audience

The only difference between speaking to one person and speaking to a large audience is more people. According to the pros, you will more genuinely connect with an audience of any size if you speak as if you were speaking to one person. So pretend you are chatting with your best friend James or Sally, and somewhere along the way they learned to clone themselves and are now filling the seats of the auditorium. This works.

494. Visit Someone in The Slammer

The worst part about prison is the lack of love. More than loneliness and the limited rights and freedoms, going without (meaningful) intimate connection with another human is true punishment. Everyone (regardless of the mistakes they have made) is worthy of love, attention and compassion. Ask yourself: *what would Jesus / Muhammed / Buddha / Krishna / The Flying Spaghetti Monster do?*

495. Tap Your Worries Away

There are a few ways to go about it. One is with your feet (put on your dancing shoes and tap the night away). The other is 'energy psychology' wherein you tap the pressure points on your body while essentially brainwashing your inner self with positive affirmations. For those who discriminate, the *Emotional Freedom Technique* is basically pseudoscience, but so are most alternative healing practices that seem to help people. Or try 'no-cebos' (the opposite of placebos).

496. Ollie

Pop, slide and jump all at the same time and you and your skateboard will perform an 'ollie' leaping into the air (and over various obstacles or gaps in the pavement). When you graduate from this (trademarked) basis of other tricks to doing a kick-flip you will be welcome at the skate park. Intrigued? Protect your precious self with full body armor.

497. Dance on Your Head

It all began when James Brown got down in 1969 with his hit *"Get on the Good Foot"*. This high-energy acrobatic dance style caught on with the kids in New York City and the rest is history. Exploding in the 1980's, breakdancing has since evolved into what you know (and dislike / love) about it today. Yes, you have to be nimble. Yes, you have to be quick. Just because you are retired doesn't mean you have to be a stick-in-the-mud. Check out YouTube for some inspiration.

498. Make a Balloon Animal

A perennial party favorite, twisting up a balloon monkey, giraffe or dog will delight everyone. Get some #260 balloons (essential balloon zoo keeper's raw material) and learn the basic twist, lock twist and fold twist. If you get good at this (and you like kids) you may have found your calling. It's never too late.

499. Keep Your Thoughts To Yourself

Don't worry if everyone is reading your mind; they are. Yet you can keep *The Total Human Elimination Movement* (T.H.E.M) at bay with 100 feet of tinfoil, a stapler, and some scotch tape from your Christmas box. Making your own tinfoil hat may or may not work for you, but it's worth a try: perhaps armed with your militia-inspired conspiracy-theory 'necessity' you will no doubt *"live long and prosper."*

500. Protest

Without the solidarity marches, peaceful demonstrations and raucous riots to voice our opinions and protect / include / value our rights and freedoms, we would be even further down the dark rabbit hole than we are now. The people united will never be defeated, so viva warranted civil disobedience!

501. Vote

Most people complain about the ways of the world, yet don't do anything about it. Perhaps establishing mandatory voting would help (but then the people pulling the strings would have to refrain from rigging elections to further their seemingly-diabolical aims). Either way, the best you can do is drop the ballot in the box and have your opinion counted (even if you don't). Consider it practice for when the Rebel Alliance establishes your colony in a galaxy far, far away on a planet yet-to-be-discovered.

502. Adopt a Pet

The bad news: 1.2 million dogs and 1.4 million cats are euthanized every year. The good news: 1.2 million dogs and 1.4 million cats are adopted each year. Thanks to opening half-way houses to unwanted / stray furry friends, the 'problem' is half-way-solved. Please spay and neuter your pet friends so the good news spreads.

503. Give Blood

Some would say the only person who gets a kick out of you giving blood is the vampire disguised as a nurse who gives you a juice box and a cookie in exchange for your donation. To others, draining their veins for the benefit of others is an annual affair (they are so eager to donate they schedule the ritual blood-letting on their calendars months in advance). Volunteerism is one thing; elective needle jabs are another (mosquitos get their fill every summer). Guilty conscience? Drive your friend to the Blood Bank and wait in the car.

504. Give Everything To Charity

Shackled by possessions? Claustrophobic to mounting clutter? If cleaning / organizing / alphabetizing / storing / insuring / moving the stuff you rarely use is stressing you out, minimalism is freedom. The less you need, the happier you will be. Don't believe it? Try it and see.

505. Host a Fondue Party

Send out the invites; consult a recipe; pick up and prepare the ingredients; melt the cheese and dip the cubes of fresh, crusty rustic bread into the pot; heat the cooking oil and deep-fry tempura-battered vegetables; melt the chocolate and dunk your strawberries, brownies, soft marshmallows and bananas; concoct a caramel sauce and plunge in the pineapple (or anything else that tastes good drenched in sweet browned butter and sugar).

506. Strip

At your age, the nudie bar would rather have you waiting on tables than up on stage. But that doesn't mean you can't perform a strip tease for your one-and-only in the bedroom. Choose some suggestive / naughty / dainty lingerie then turn down the lights and push play on some suggestive / naughty / dainty music. And don't stop there; make it a regular event.

507. Cut Down a Tree

Don't cheat and use a chainsaw. If you can swing an axe, make like a lumberjack and use that. Learn how to sharpen your axe before you start swinging Paul Bunyan, and you will get a work-out like never before. Invigorated? Buck it all up, stack it and season it for next winter. Wood: the fuel that heats you twice (or however many times you struggled to get it from its natural state into your fireplace).

508. Talk to a Homeless Person

Regardless of what you've seen on the news, heard on the radio, or read in the papers: they don't bite (many folks living on the street don't have any teeth). If you can't imagine having a conversation with another human being who simply made different choices, give them your doggie bag of leftovers when you pass them on the street. Keep in mind that people with little to give are often the most generous.

509. Pick Up Someone's Litter

Go to the dollar store and pick up some garbage bags, rubber gloves, and one of those things with the handle and trigger and claws. Stay off the side of the highway, or you might be mistaken for a convict on work detail (and encourage passersby to give you more work to do). Even though it may seem like people don't care, everyone appreciates a clean neighborhood, public beach and city park. This author's irreverent mother likes to joke:*"You will get your reward in heaven."*

510. Dress Up as Santa

Fat? Bearded? Happy? Perfect. As long as you don't scrimp on a suit, the kids will love you (they can smell a phony). The more believable you are as the iconic symbol *"around which the entire kid year revolves"* the less you will have to dry clean your suit (you know why). What could fill your ears with holiday cheer quicker than all the squealing glee?

511. Send a Care Package

Did anyone ever send you a care package? Students holed up at college or soldiers far away defending our freedom would love some extra attention. TLC endears you to the recipient of your gift (but you aren't looking for praise). Wrap up a few goodies and ship them off to kin or close friend. You don't even have to bake; if it's above freezing at your package's destination, chocolate chip cookies always melt in the mouth of someone special.

512. Get Revenge

What has been done to you that can be undone (or made right) by getting even? Be careful: it's possible you could (unintentionally) overcompensate in your attempt to balance the scales. FYI: the perpetrator has likely forgotten all about you (and the infraction in question) while you are stuck stewing in poison and obsessed about leveling the playing field.

513. Go Caroling

By the time December 1st rolls around you may already be applying for a reindeer hunting license and a one-way ticket to Florida for a certain snowman. Whether you like it or not, Christmas songs have been tattooed on your mind (and no matter how talented the brain surgeon, you will never get them removed). So why not join in the sub-zero door-to-door fun and sing your heart out. You don't think you know the words, but you do.

514. Teach a Class

You have probably forgotten more about your favorite subject than some people know about it. If you can celebrate the successes (and reframe the failures) of your students (regardless of age) you will be loved by all. Develop a curriculum and/or course and get it listed on your local community center's continuing education calendar. Those who cannot do, teach.

515. Write to a Politician

Do you know the 'sandwich' model of giving feedback? This approach has 3 parts (like a sandwich). You begin with a slice of fresh bread (a sincere compliment or *"well-done"*). Now slap on the processed meat and a squirt of hot mustard (make a suggestion or offer an alternate point-of-view). Now top it all off with another slice of bread (acknowledge the politician's ability / past accomplishments). Do this, and you can consider your personal / professional / political aims all-but-achieved (or at least voiced and heard).

516. Get a Library Card

Without access to the free tomes covering everything from aardvark to zyxt (the obsolete second-person singular present-tense spelling of the word 'see') you would not be reading this book. The library is your BFF that will stick around long after your other BFFs have bailed.

517. Volunteer at Hospice

Chronically- / terminally- / seriously-ill patients find much-needed respite in hospice care, where their emotional and spiritual needs are the focus. If you have ever had first-hand experience with hospice care, you know the value it brings to those nearing the end of their lives. Attending to the specific needs of the dying is an uncommon calling; one that may resonate with you.

518. Host a Radio Show

Do you love music? Have you always wanted to be a DJ? Now is your chance. There are thousands of campus and community radio stations (which means there are a few not too far from you). Attend a volunteer orientation; learn the ropes; and you will be riding the air waves playing / curating / sharing your favorite sounds like never before. If you have the desire, you can do it.

519. Join a Coven

Not presently versed in the dark arts? Not to worry: there are 200,000 people (in the US alone) who dabble in magic in one form or another. So if you've always wondered what was lurking in the shadows of the 4th dimension (or what Aunt Hattie really thinks of your new husband) find yourself a coven. And when you get invited to the next seance, don't leave home without your garlic talisman.

519. Take Riding Lessons

All ages and skills are welcome. Learn and practice tacking up, untacking, jumping, vaulting, dressing, grooming, Western and English style riding; plus horse and tack care in your private or group lesson. Don't have your own horse? No problem; chances are you can rent one for the day. Giddy up!

521. Take a First Aid Course

How are you in an emergency? Could you save someone's life if their life depended on it?

Everyone should know basic cardiopulmonary resuscitation (CPR). If it's been a while since your last certification, brush up on your skills with a refresher course. Now that you're retired, you don't have to worry about work-related injuries and illnesses, because work is history. Looking ahead, having some first aid skills up your sleeve could prove useful at home, abroad, in the bush, or even at sea.

522. Belly Dance

Before you start shaking your bootie, keep in mind the basis of belly dancing: you are not supposed to shake your bootie. You bootie will shake on its own when you command your tummy muscles to do your belly's bidding. Sequins, scarves and swords await you in this torso-taming Middle Eastern folk dance. Yallah!

523. Learn to Write Left–Handed

Thanks to neuroplasticity, *"your brain's ability to reorganize itself by forming new neural connections throughout your life"*, you *can* teach yourself new tricks. Fancy being ambidextrous with a pen, instead of just unconsciously channeling the wisdom of your non-conscious mind via left-handed written responses to your conscious brain-posed questions? Practice will bring you as close to perfection as human nature will allow.

524. Take an Art Class

Have you ever joked at an art opening that you could have painted the same thing in your sleep? Arrogance is ignorance, smarty pants. Even if you are not guilty of said crime, you may be guilty of ignoring this classic advice offered by well-meaning loved ones if you have ever dreamed of 'being creative'. The challenge (as when looking at anything 'old') is to see it for the first time.

525. Join a Book Club

The benefits of a book club include (but are not limited to): Friendship (you will forge lifetime connections with like-minded people); conversation (covering topics of interest to you and your biddies); self-expression (finally a forum where you can tell it like it is); expansion of your literary horizons (being open to various interpretations of the books you read); and finally, good food (end the evening with a potluck).

526. Learn How to Write Code

If you are anything like this author, coding and programming are beyond your grasp. Just as Pete Seeger sang in the 1950's, there is a season for dinosaur eggs and a season for alien babies. You know who you are. And if you don't, that's what this book is for.

527. Host a Podcast

Just like a radio show (but online and available 24/7/365) and covering every imaginable topic you could think of, there is something for everyone. The simplest set-up requires little more than a microphone; audio editing software; and something to say. What? Not ready to spam the airwaves with your rants and raves? Being a guest on someone else's podcast is the next best thing (but this won't happen unless you have something to say).

528. Lucid Dream

Have you ever had a dream that felt more real than this moment right now? With countless realities existing simultaneously in the span of space and time, even a brief glimpse of what was really going on would fry your noodle. Could you use a little objective perspective on your life? Train yourself to 'wake up' in the middle of a dream and take a look around.

529. Build or Repair Computers

Much simpler than writing software, any mechanically-minded engineer-type can build and/or repair a computer. Fascinated by the inner workings of these insanely-powerful machines? This is only the beginning. What do you want a computer to do that it doesn't do already? Pull one apart or start from scratch and change the trajectory of humanity forever.

530. Be a Guinea Pig

Are you running in circles like a hamster on a wheel waiting to donate your body to science? Get a kick out of your retirement while you are still alive and participate in a human trial instead. The developers of experimental drugs and procedures froth at the mouth to get their hands on non-animal test subjects like you. But watch out: if you feel the sudden urge to peel your probing doctor's face off (and he or she turns out to be a lizard) don't ask questions. Run!

531. Write a Letter to The Editor

How often do you want the last word on a story in the paper? If the answer is *"all the time"* you have likely already written a letter to the editor and seen your critique of the issue on the op-ed (opposite-the-editorial) page. Was that the sad end of it? Are your heavily-researched conspiratorial discourses suddenly being ignored? Find an alternative platform to voice your opinions.

532. Change a Flat Tire

As long as you don't pull a 'Ralphie' and utter the mother of all curse words in the presence of your hypocritical father and end up blind from soap poisoning, changing a tire is relatively easy, and will boost your confidence and fuel you with enough courage to perhaps attempt changing a light bulb (which for some reason is 10x more difficult to some people). Changing someone else's tire? If it's your lucky day, they might just need a jump too.

533. Learn a Poem by Heart

Whose wily wit, wicked wisdom and way-with-words weaves wonder into your weekend wherever you wander? Silvia Plath, Rumi, Robert Frost, William Shakespeare, Emily Dickinson, Walt Whitman, Tagore? The list is endless (everyone is a poet nowadays) so pick your favorite piece of prose and learn to recite it (you never know when this skill will come in handy).

534. Start a Collection

Stamps, coins, bottle caps, feathers, pigs, hot sauce, ugly sweaters, antiques, classic cars, guitars, typewriters, ornaments, spools of thread, travel tags, photos, garden nomes, hair brushes, beer, wine, vintage clothing, books, kitchen utensils, ceramics, doll houses, bird feeders, doorknobs, shoes, handbags, spoons, phone books or magazines. At the very least, having a lot of the same stuff in one place will force you to get organized.

535. Finish a Crossword Puzzle

Finishing the most-difficult crossword puzzle in the NY Times, 10 letters (solution at the end of the paragraph). If you want to get good at crossword puzzles (and you can resist the urge to cheat) you will ultimately accomplish a task that to most people seems (the solution): monumental.

536. Volunteer at The Food Bank

You don't even want to know how many people don't have enough 'food' to eat (packaged, processed sweetened / salted sawdust is not food). With fresh fruits and vegetables growing everywhere (and waters full of swimming staples and various other delicacies) there is no reason for anyone to go hungry. But for those who can't access these fields, farms and fresh / salty waters (nor the grocery store) the food bank is church (where good samaritans are always welcome).

537. Buy a Franchise

With hundreds (if not thousands) to choose from, turn-key businesses are a tried-and-true way to feel like an entrepreneur without the blood, sweat and tears. With enough money, you can buy your way into any business or industry and hire a seasoned management team to run the show so you can get back to sweating, bleeding and crying about the things that really matter to you.

538. Take Voice Lessons

Sing: la-la-la-la-la-la-la. Now a step (tone) higher: la-la-la-la-la-la-la. Learning to breathe; project your voice; train your ear; adopt a new style; and/or expand your repertoire are outcomes both professionals and enthusiasts alike seek in their singing lessons. Any of these fortes sound pitch-perfect to you? Step out of the shower and bare your soul; angels don't need towels.

539. Go Mountain Biking

Don't go and buy a summer pass at your local ski hill until the training wheels are off. Find a few trails to go pedaling in peace and earn your stripes; you risk major injury on the downhill slalom course (even with full body armor). Your humble steed has much to do with your enjoyment of this perfect marriage of bicycles and the outdoors, so opt for full-suspension come graduation day.

540. Go to Your School Reunion

Have you changed in 40 years? Wouldn't it be neat to go back in time and see just how much? Aren't you curious to see who you married (and divorced) who? How about verifying if the person voted 'most likely to succeed' actually did? Unfortunately, these are questions social media just can't answer; you must see the past with your own eyes.

541. Decorate Someone with Body Paint

Avoid the nooks-and-crannies (unless the body paint is of the edible, non-toxic variety, in which case it's like dessert following a long, hard day in front of the easel). For the nth time (as in most subjects) there are no rules when adorning someone with body paint, except enjoying yourselves. The colors, designs and textures you draw on will make drawing on your living canvas such a ticklishly creative escapade that you may just give up and eat dessert first.

542. Sign a Petition

It doesn't always seem like your voice or opinion count (but few things are as they seem). Adding your signature to a list of fellow concerned citizens in favor of (or in opposition to) some legislation is not only a symbol of solidarity with like-minded radicals, but also a sworn oath (of sorts) to a cause you believe in.

543. Dress Up for The Rocky Horror Picture Show

Both a parody and a tribute to both science fiction and horror movies, this musical comedy-horror film has given theater-goers permission ever since its release in 1975 to dress up like their favorite characters and toss props like toast, confetti and toilet paper around the theater. The staff loves it.

544. Enjoy a Colorful Christmas

Never hiked through the woods in knee-deep snow to cut down your own Christmas tree? Have yet to sip piña coladas under a thatched roof while the warm ocean breeze soothes you to sleep? Ever listened to the rain on the roof nestled snugly in the rainforest? Or picked thorns out of your caboose after sliding down a sand dune before losing your mind from all the stars in the desert? Take your pick; it's up to you: white, green, brown or blue.

545. Take an Improv Acting Class

Do you have a funny bone hiding somewhere? Nothing will tickle it like improv. Whether you muster the courage to get up on stage after an 8-week course (or opt to watch from the sidelines) you will have the time of your life, even if you didn't think you were funny. If you can think and talk and move your body, you will have a blast doing improv.

546. Write to a Celebrity

There is no guarantee your favorite celebrity will read your dissertation or screenplay, but that doesn't mean you shouldn't write to them. If you are lucky to get a response, don't be surprised if it's an 8x10 chicken-scratch sharpie-scrawl that looks like it was signed by a vandal with a degree in hieroglyphics. Better yet, pen a note to your now-80-year-old teen heartthrob and you have a much better chance of receiving a sincere reply.

547. Pretend to Be Disabled

The Scandinavian flick *The Idiots* says it all. A group of students (conveniently living together) go out on the town pretending they are disabled. Ultimately, the sky comes crumbling down when the ethics of their social experiment come into question. It begs the question: why is it so easy to be kind to people with visible disabilities, yet not extend this unconditional kindness to everyone else?

548. Sell Something You Made

There is only one way to know if what you made has value to someone other than your best friend or doting spouse (both of whom are one-eyed). Ask someone with no investment in your emotional well-being whatsoever to trade you money for your creation. Fret not; people buy the strangest things, so don't shrivel up into a ball of worry if your something doesn't immediately fly off the shelf at the farmer's market.

549. Go to The Opera

You (will) either love opera or hate it (there is no in-between). At the very least, you will enjoy dressing up; admiring the costumes, sets and props; appreciating the music. If you're not sure divas belting out arias in foreign languages are your cup of tea, sneak in some booze to entertain yourself. Maybe you'll get a tour of the orchestra pit after hob-nobbing with the upper-crust (which is why you went in the first place).

550. Request a Song on The Radio

When your favorite radio station's 'listener line' isn't being abused by contest contestants, call them up and request your favorite song. You could even email / text / tweet your plea for your chosen tune, maybe even introducing the DJ to new (or old) music while you're at it. Stick to the show format (don't ask a country-rock station to play a children's song) and sit back and relax (or spark a mini mosh pit).

551. Write a Poem

Be assured your words don't have to rhyme or follow a particular tempo or meter (heck, you can play with characters, tenses and perspective throughout verse and stanza). Bob "Happy Little Trees" Ross from *The Joy of Painting* was fond of parlaying the following advice: *"This is your world."* Take his advice; poetry is no exception.

552. Chase a Tornado

Your motives for pursuing a tornado likely vary from others interested in the same (insane) activity. Are you simply curious, or are you conducting scientific experiments like Doc Brown in the *Back To The Future* series? Perhaps you thrive on harnessing extreme weather phenomena for your own benefit (like going back in time). But don't go too far, because like *Dorothy* you will inevitably realize *"there's no place like home."* And who would feed *Toto* while you're gone?

553. Get Your Handwriting Analyzed

What do all the bumps / creases / lines / blemishes on the palm of your hand mean? Just because your mitts are maps that reveal unlikely clues to your destiny doesn't mean the characteristics of your palms have anything to do with what your handwriting says about you. Don't pay someone too much for their analysis; you can sate yourself with everything you have ever wanted to know by going to the library or typing 'handwriting analysis' into *Google* and reading what countless experts have to say.

554. Re-Create Your Family Tree

If you haven't been pruned from the family tree (or cactus) yet (and/or your nearest and dearest are as bland and as boring as a garden weed) why not grow your own forest or orchard? But this time, instead of using people's names, try filling the branches with your clan's scandals, foolish improprieties and unscrupulous hijinks. What fun!

555. Bury a Time Capsule

How would you like to be remembered? What items, objects, ideas or keepsakes are meaningful to you? Giving future generations a glimpse into the past via your collection of public and private treasures is a gift they will cherish for years to come. Lock it all in a special box, bury it somewhere, and make sure you leave clues to its exact location (lest you would prefer it fall into alien tentacles light years from now).

3 Things To Do Next... If You Want:

1. Write a review to enlighten your peers:
   https://www.amazon.com/dp/0994846843

2. Connect with the author. Send your praise or flame to: oliverlukedelorie@gmail.com

3. Stay in the loop and join the book club. The future is bright at: thejoyofretiring.com

Also By The Author

Dear Leroy

The Cat Way

Money Magic

The Magic of Music

The Law of Reaction

Secrets of Successful Students

100 Small Ways To Manage Time

100 Small Ways To Quit Worrying

How To Find What You Never Lost

Shinrin Yoku - The Art of Forest Bathing

Wabi Sabi - Finding Beauty in Imperfection

www.ingramcontent.com/pod-product-compliance
Lightning Source LLC
Chambersburg PA
CBHW070800280326
41934CB00012B/2987

www.ingramcontent.com/pod-product-compliance
Lightning Source LLC
Chambersburg PA
CBHW062036270326
41929CB00014B/2444